The New Modern Aesthetic

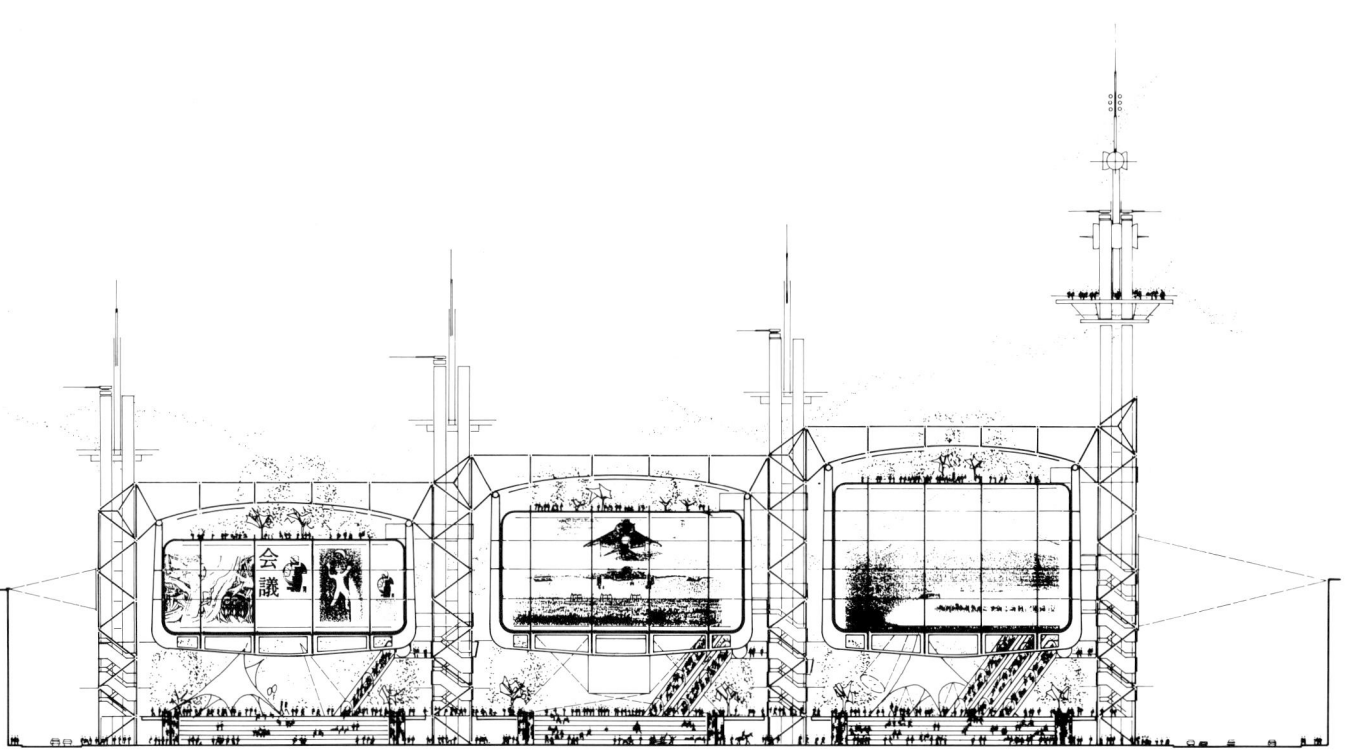

RICHARD ROGERS, TOKYO FORUM COMPETITION

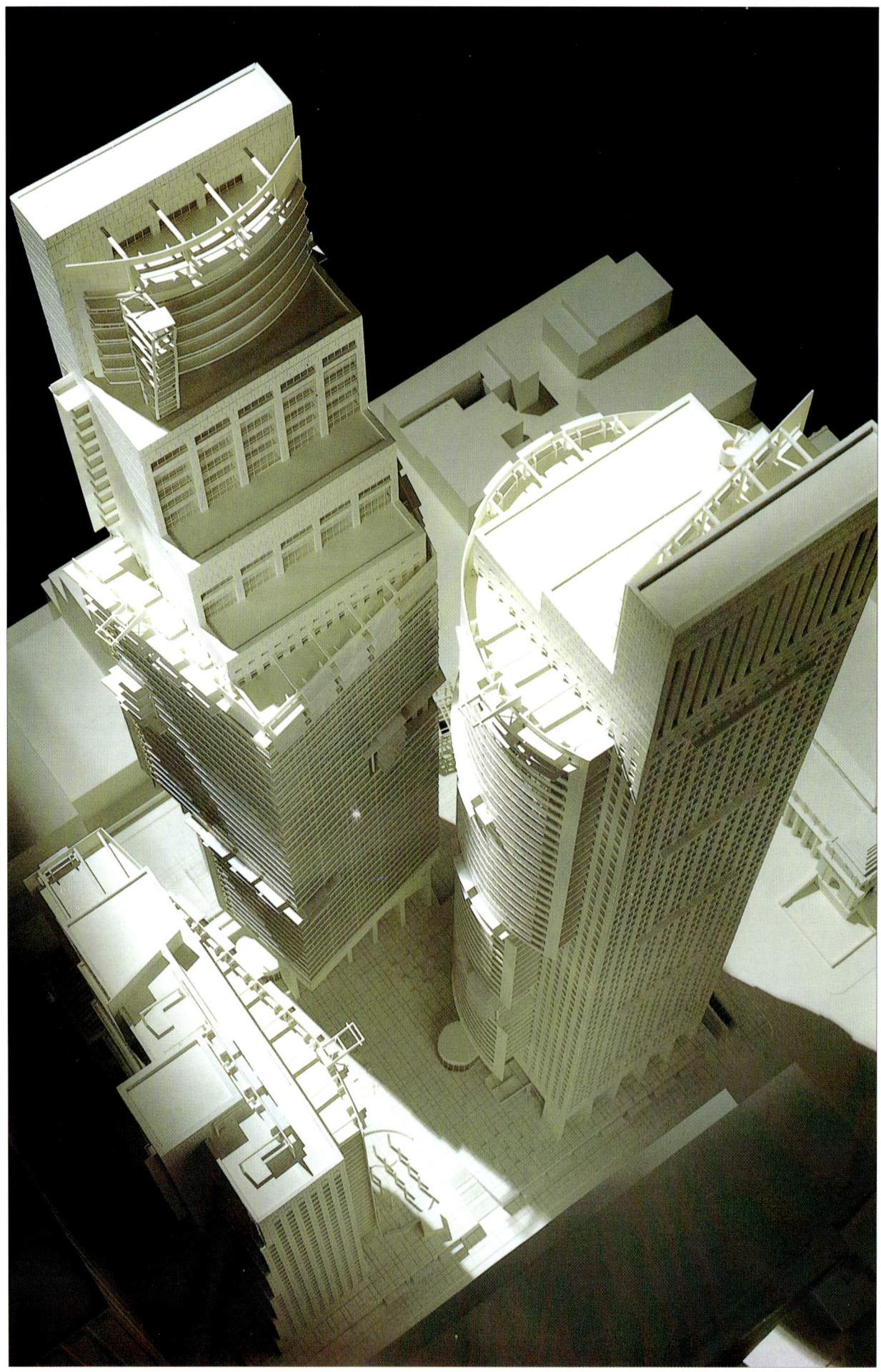

RICHARD MEIER, MADISON SQUARE TOWERS
PHOTO BY ESTO

An Architectural Design Profile

The New Modern Aesthetic

BRANSON COATES, BOHEMIA JAZZ CAFE

ACADEMY EDITIONS • LONDON / ST. MARTIN'S PRESS • NEW YORK

Acknowledgements:
The theme of this issue is taken from two events: The International Symposium at the Tate Gallery and The Second Annual
Architecture Forum at the Royal Institution. Both events were organised by The Academy Forum.
We would like to thank the directors and personnel of the Royal Institution and of the Tate Gallery, particularly Richard Humphries
of the Education Department, for providing us with a venue for the Symposium and David Lambert for video taping the event.We
would like to express our thanks to the October Gallery and Jose Ferez for mounting the concurrent exhibition of Richard Meier
Collages. In addition we would like to thank the participants who came from all over the world, and Marshall Berman who, whilst
unable to attend, wrote his contribution at such short notice. We are particularly grateful to the chairmen Paul Finch, Jonathan
Glancey and Christopher Martin and to the architects who contributed pieces to this issue.

Publications:
The New Moderns by Charles Jencks
Richard Meier – Buildings and Projects
Tadao Ando An Architectural Monograph
Richard Meier Collages
Philosophy & Architecture Journal of Philosophy & the Visual Arts Vol 1 No 2
New Architecture Architectural Design no 3/4 1990

The Photographic Credits:
Pavillon de L'Arsenal – collages of La Grande Arche.
Esto Photographics – all photographs for Richard Meier
Gaston Bergeret – photographs for Odile Decq and Benoit Cornette.
American Center in Paris for Frank Gehry interview and material.
Paul Warchol & Edward Valentine Hames – photographs for Branson Coates.
All other illustrations and photographs are provided by the architects.

EDITOR
Dr Andreas C Papadakis

EDITORIAL OFFICES: 42 LEINSTER GARDENS, LONDON W2 3AN TELEPHONE: 071-402 2141
HOUSE EDITOR: Maggie Toy DESIGNED BY: Andrea Bettella, Mario Bettella SUBSCRIPTIONS MANAGER: Mira Joka
Editorial staff contributing to this issue: Vivian Constantinopoulos and Julia Schoelkopf

CONSULTANTS: Catherine Cooke, Dennis Crompton, Terry Farrell, Kenneth Frampton, Charles Jencks
Heinrich Klotz, Leon Krier, Robert Maxwell, Demetri Porphyrios, Colin Rowe, Derek Walker

First published in Great Britain in 1990 by *Architectural Design*
an imprint of the
ACADEMY GROUP LTD, 7 HOLLAND STREET, LONDON W8 4NA
ISBN: 1-85490-043-9 (UK)

Architectural Design Profile 86 is published as part of *Architectural Design* Vol 60 7-8/1990
Published in the United States of America by
ST MARTIN'S PRESS, 175 FIFTH AVENUE, NEW YORK 10010
ISBN: 0-312-06031-9 (USA)

Printed and bound in Singapore

Contents

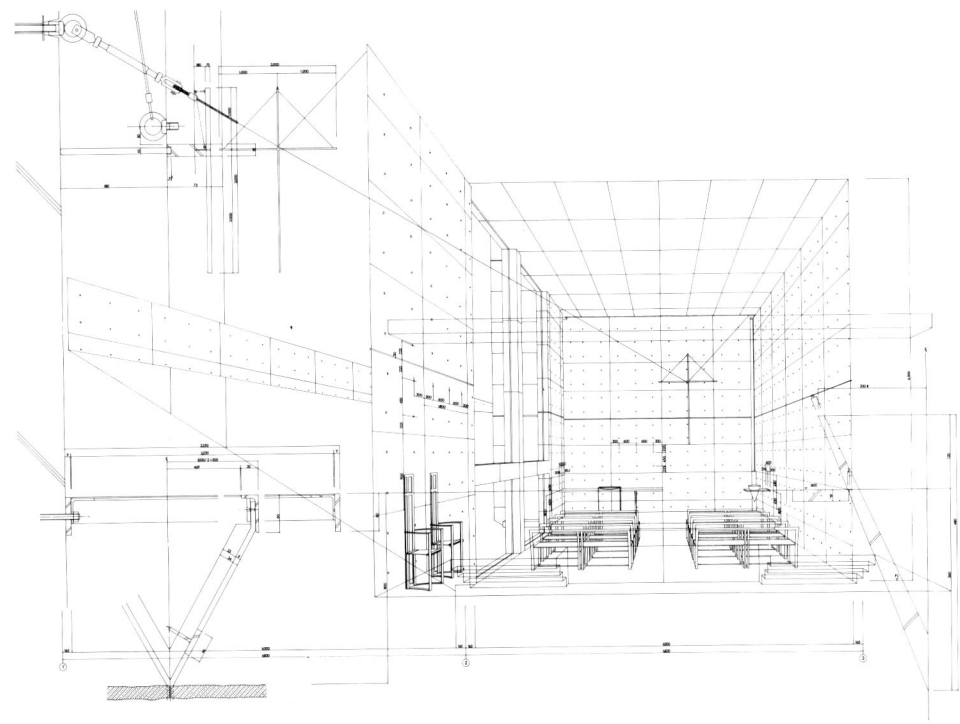

TADAO ANDO, CHAPEL ON MOUNT ROKKO, SECTIONAL PERSPECTIVE

**The Second Annual Architectural Forum at the Royal Institute
The New Modern Symposium at the Tate Gallery**

L'ARCHE DE LA DÉFENSE, COLLAGE

ANDREAS PAPADAKIS
THE QUESTION OF MODERNISM

The question asked here and at the Tate Gallery symposium is whether there really is a New Modern architecture today and, if so, what directions it will pursue. It can be argued that Post-Modernism, since its beginnings in the late seventies when pioneer architects reacted against Modernism, succeeded not so much in destroying Modernism but in bringing about changes that made it more palatable to today's new thinking. Clearly, if Modernism was to succeed in becoming once again the leading movement of the day, it had to counter the objections expressed most eloquently by Tom Wolfe. It needed to rethink its worship of heroes long dead, and re-establish a continuity with the past; to abandon its love affair with new materials and adjust to the social conditions of today. In other words, Post-Modernism offered a way in which the new Modernism could hold its own in the sophisticated nineties, which demand not only quality of life but a theoretical justification for it. No one would have expected a New Modernism with a theoretical content to develop in the Anglo-Saxon world, with its innate fear of theory; indeed it needed the Gallic training and tenacity of Bernard Tschumi, who for years battled for an architecture based on theory, and the intuitive talents of Peter Eisenman, an architect in search of a theory, to develop one strand based on the philosophy of Deconstruction and now that theory is respectable, even in the Anglo-Saxon world, their work shows perhaps the most imaginative direction in architecture today, rich in an imagery alluding to a futuristic world that has captured the imagination of institutional clients and students alike. Eisenman's Wexner Center was preceded by Tschumi's pavilions in the Parc de la Villette in Paris and it is also in Paris the Arc de Triomphe, built to celebrate long-forgotten Napoleonic victories, is no longer meaningful whereas the new Arche de la Défense, built by a young Scandinavian architect, has caught the imagination of today's Parisians. Deconstruction was discussed with Bernard Tschumi and Peter Eisenman at an earlier symposium at the Tate Gallery just over a year ago. Today we can look at it afresh with Daniel Libeskind who is at present building the Jewish Museum in Berlin. The strands of New Modernism are many, including hi-tech, a very British architecture that is both evocative and practical in the hands of such architects as Richard Rogers and Sir Norman Foster, but it has a drawback as a candidate for New Modern architecture in that it has been in existence since Victorian times, but even so still reflects the future. Today the discussion is in a broader context and we have the opportunity to examine the contribution of Richard Meier whose designs for the Getty Museum in California are approaching completion, and to discuss an overall definition of the New Modernism, including the contribution of the Japanese architect Tadao Ando. The discussion surrounds not whether there is a New Modernism, but whether Deconstruction is part of the Modern in Post-Modernism. The final word may already have been said in Berlin in the form of a new book entitled Eine postmoderne Moderne.

MARSHALL BERMAN
WHERE ARE THE NEW MODERNS ?

'All that is solid melts into air' proclaimed Marx, and over a century later, Marshall Berman takes this phrase as a point from which to view the modern world. This world has undergone significant changes and the strands of Modernism have been ever different. Berman examines the way in which these differences have evolved – what can now be constituted as modern? The author draws on two words to expound on his personal viewpoints: Modernism – that of architecture and also the world of visual art and literature, and modernisation – the changes that have taken place in the capitalist Western world. These two phenomena are inextricably linked; both an impetus, one for the other, and both conditions of modern life, where, as Jean-Jacques Rousseau had his young protagonist state in the novel The New Eloise, '. . . a continuing flux and reflux of prejudices and conflicting opinions . . . Everyone constantly places himself in contradiction with himself . . . everything is absurd, but nothing is shocking, because everyone is accustomed to everything.' Modern sensibility begins with feelings such as these, full of paradoxes and contradictions, and this is exactly what Berman scrutinises and analyses, charting all the ironies which amalgamate to form modernity. Moreover, Berman succeeds in making a valuable contribution to the social implications of the pair Modernism and modernisation. He cites a number of figures through the past, both real and fictional, to depict the social and human effects of modern life, and, as he says, all of these 'are moved at once by the will to change – to transform both themselves and their world – and by a terror of disorientation and disintegration, of life falling apart. They all know the thrill and the dread of a world in which "all that is solid melts into air"'. Marshall Berman was invited to participate in the discussion at the Forum on 'The New Moderns' which he was unable to attend. However, a number of conversations with Andreas Papadakis resulted in the piece produced here. Modernism for Berman is realism, and although we may be appalled by it, regarding ourselves as anti-modern, we still have to fight it in order to come to terms with it. The irony of battling against the modern world is paradigmatic of modern man showing an attempt at change and, more importantly, progress so true to this very real condition; and, as Berman has stated, 'This will not resolve the contradictions that pervade modern life; but it should help us to understand them, so that we can be clear and honest in facing and working through the forces that make us what we are.' [Ed]

As the author of a big book on the traditions of Modernism, I'm an interested party. I felt hurt and angry all through the 1980s, when people said Modernism was dead. Now, in the 1990s, as people are discovering that Modernism still has plenty to say, I need to restrain myself from saying, 'See, I told you so'.

Andreas Papadakis offers a short list of 'New Moderns': Eisenman, Tschumi, Libeskind, Meier, Foster, Rogers. Do these people constitute a coherent 'New Modern' movement? I don't know. But then, the 'Old Modern' movement wasn't so coherent either, especially if we remember to include names like Wright, Aalto, Taut and Mendelssohn, Tatlin and Leonidov. More important than coherence is the structure of feeling that Charles Jencks calls 'yearning for a *new* movement'. This yearning itself deserves looking into, because it is a desire for some alternative to the spirit of the 1980s.

The most important thing about the 1980s, in the USA and Britain, is so obvious we often forget it: it was the age of Thatcher and Reagan. Its dominant social policy was a massive redistribution of wealth upwards from the poor to the rich. (As my daughter's old T-shirt puts it, 'From the needy to the greedy') Governments helped capital reconfigure itself in a way that combined financial boom with industrial collapse. This new order caught the non-capitalists off-guard. Millions of industrial workers were laid off, their plants moved or closed, their unions increasingly helpless, their political power *kaput*. The labour force swelled above and below them, in high finance and fast food. There were many celebrations of free enterprise, but in fact the international drug traffic was the only medium in which this freedom meant something real.

In the built environments of the 1980s, Wall Streets metastasised everywhere while factory towns became ghost towns. Urban public services, deprived of state support, generally deteriorated (except in the financial districts, which raised private money), and public architecture virtually ceased to exist. Meanwhile, private real estate developers seized the day, usually with the help of massive (and artfully hidden) government subsidies. The new generation of big buildings – corporate headquarters, office and apartment towers, luxurious shopping arcades – towered over the old ones, and blotted out the sky; on the ground they obliterated tenements and welfare hotels, and put poor people out on the streets. Architects concentrated on serving their corporate clients. If they had any reservations about what they were building, or proposing to build, they kept it to themselves and cried – or maybe elegaically sighed all the way to the bank.

Post-Modern culture inadvertently helped all this happen. Born in the 1960s, amid the gravities of the Great Society, Post-Modern irreverence and irony at first offered a breath of fresh air. But Post-Modernism didn't change, and didn't respond to the changes around it, and twenty years later, in the Reagan-Thatcher ambience, it helped pollute the air. Even as right wing governments were fighting to destroy the whole public sector, Post-Modern thinkers were using all their intellectual power to discredit public education and public health. While television producers, real estate developers and admen outdid each other in creating seductive surfaces and glitzy facades, Post-Modern architects and designers told us that it was silly for us to want anything real behind our facades – indeed, that words like 'real' could only be used in quotes, with irony – and that the play of surfaces was all that there was in the world. The Post-Modern pursuit of happiness seemed to abandon any attempts to live in a true or just or authentic way; its one thing needful was to know all the prevailing semiotic codes, so as to enjoy the infinite possibilities of interpretive play.

After a generation of this, many people are sick of the play. One of the things they are saying is that they want a *New* Modernism. But I suspect what they're after isn't so much a particular look, sound or style: it's a culture that's serious, that wants to discover and express what's real. Not that it's clear what *is* real, or how we can ever answer such a question. But there are lots of people out there who want an architecture – or an art or music or a literature or a social theory – that at least will search for ways to ask. You could call it an architecture that *cares*.

The late 1980s offer two stirring examples of an architecture that cares: Norman Foster's Hong Kong and Shanghai Bank building in Hong Kong, and Johan Spreckelsen's Arche de la Défense in Paris. Both works point very insistently towards the future, as in the coming millenium, but also the very concrete, chronologically near future, as in Hong Kong's 1997 and Paris' 1992. The Hong Kong building (I haven't actually seen it, but I've looked at many pictures) seems extravagantly risky, in geological as well as political ways. Who knows what the Chinese will do with it in 1997 when they take over? Who even knows how long it will stand up? The trusses that support it emphasise rather than hide its vulnerability. Its size, density, monumental solidity and high-tech style, all evoke an idea of immense and dangerous enterprise – something like a space shuttle that could blow up any minute, and take us all with it as it goes down. The building looks at once sacred and dynamic, kind of like Vladimir Tatlin's unbuilt monument to the Communist International. Indeed, we could see this bank as a monument to a capitalist international, proclaiming to the world, Behold! in the final conflict, capitalism has won. But what kind of capitalism? A kind that at any moment could crash! This bank is a self–monument to the purest form of rich capitalism. Its grand self-doubt brings us the latest mode of the capitalist sublime.

Meanwhile in Mitterrand's Paris, in the city's newest triumphal arch, we are faced with (and I've seen this one in the flesh) a kind of democratic sublime. With its cubist form and angles, and its computer imagery and space-age materials, this arch presents a vision that has been often imagined, but very rarely embodied: a fusion of the 20th-century's avant-garde science with its avant-garde art. The arch looks so fine, in such an instantly classic way, that a spectator can't help but wonder why works of this stature and quality are so rare. One answer may be that democratic socialism is the only political system likely to even try to fuse aesthetic sensitivity, scientific knowledge, adventurousness, and the desire and talent to plan for society as a whole. Still, few social democratic regimes have ever tried it. Socialism usually comes to power at moments of economic crisis, and for reasons of democratic politics it is generally locked into narrow nationalism. The arch is meant to make us think of 1992, Europe's magic year of integration. Who knows what will really happen? But the arch helps us imagine New Modern adventures, and even imagine that Paris could be the capital of the 21st century as it was of the 19th. Walking around the arch's neighbourhood and at La Villette, we see it's full of African and Caribbean faces, and many of them look as if they're at home. Then we remember what the modern metropolis was supposed to be, and maybe still can be. Maybe the kids climbing around the Arche de la Défense are 'The New Moderns'.

ACKERBERG HOUSE
ALL PICTURES IN THIS ARTICLE ARE BY ESTO

KENNETH FRAMPTON
RICHARD MEIER AND THE CITY IN MINIATURE

Richard Meier's work is lyrical, sensuous and striking. A lover of abstraction, he is at the same time an architect with a keen eye for function, regarding function as similar to a well-built structure. Meier's buildings are based on a clearly-defined structural grid, which nevertheless do not ignore the human, the grid being a scaling device bringing the scaling of structural elements down to human proportions; while inherent in the work is a fragmentation and a shifting of this grid. His recent design for the J Paul Getty Center in Los Angeles shows a similar thinking: cubic masses forming a series of interconnecting buildings – one building and simultaneously many. How is this sensibility akin to the spirit of the New Moderns? Kenneth Frampton talks the critical viewer through the architect's work, analysing a number of his recent projects taken from Meier's recent monograph.*

It is ironic that the American architect Richard Meier has projected some of his finest work in Europe. In these projects he has often shown how one may realise large buildings in such a way as to revitalise the existing urban pattern. So that now after years of free-standing, small to medium sized buildings, we have to acknowledge the presence of a civic capacity in Meier's work. Meier is able to perform more readily in this regard in Europe, for unlike Frank Lloyd Wright, who demonstrated in his introspective public buildings how one could compensate for the spatial/institutional 'void' of the average American provincial town, Meier's tectonic language tends to fail him when confronted with the ubiquitous motopian placelessness of the United States. This much is suggested by his recent project for the Santa Monica Beach Hotel that tries to create its own semi-urban context against the random contours of the coast and the expanse of the ocean. But despite its decisive boundary and its formalistic energy it displays none of the contextual subtlety of the proposal for the National Investment Bank in The Hague.

In my view Meier is the only convincing civic architect of the original Five Architects and the last decade has given him ample opportunity to prove his prowess in this regard. The first indication that he possessed a particular feeling for civic form surely came with his Bronx Developmental Center of 1977, but Meier was not able to follow this initiative until the High Museum, Atlanta of 1983 and the Museum of Decorative Arts, Frankfurt of 1985. While these two museums have considerable civic presence, it is regrettable that he never had a chance to realise his IBA housing scheme projected for Berlin in 1982. This low rise perimeter development, following the Landwehrkanal, was surely one of the few seminal schemes projected for IBA, in that it established a form and scale appropriate to the history of the city. It demonstrated how the Bruno Taut legacy, his Uncle Tom's Hutte or his Hufeisensiedlung, could be adapted to the centre of the city while still creating continuous street frontage and precisely defining the semi-public garden space to the rear.

It would seem that with the exception of the Ulm cultural centre, Meier has yet to realise an art gallery that, typologically speaking, is a museum rather than a large house. Thus, while Atlanta and Frankfurt display an exhilarating sense of civic presence, they are somewhat reduced as public buildings by an inappropriate sense of domesticity. This is evident say in the carpeted public ramps that are barely wide enough to allow two people to pass side by side. Fortunately, this regressive informality seems to be absent from his recent public work.

Meier has had the fortune to be recognised by continental corporate clients as an architect of world stature. This much is clear from the way in which Renault, Siemens and Pirelli have elected to commission him. Only in England has he been met with indifference. Thus, while he was an initial candidate for the Anglo-American National Gallery competition he did not make it into the final list of participants. Could it be that the trustees and their advisers did not want an architect who had the will and the evident capacity to build a decisively modern building on the site in such a way as it would harmonise with both the historic square and the existing museum?

It is equally regrettable that Meier's project for Renault at Boulogne-Billancourt will not be realised, for this was surely an exemplary study in the transformation of a disused, industrial inner urban site. Bounded on one side by the Seine and on the other by a triangular grove of trees and on the other sides by typical cross-wall city fabric, Renault was a multiple courtyard scheme transformed into a sculptural tour de force in its public head-building. Faced throughout in light-weight metal panels, Meier's Renault Complex was projected as though it were a tectonic metaphor for the automobile. This proposal was a demonstrative urban piece and had it been built, we would have had a development such as we have not seen in Paris since the pre-war urban blocks of Michel Roux-Spitz.

Meier's project for Siemens Headquarters in Munich could hardly attain the same canonical dimension since it was largely a piece of direct urban fill. However, Meier attempts to create a world in miniature, using courtyard blocks to restore a city fabric destroyed by the introduction of an underpass. As it stands the project has yet to arrive at a truly convincing treatment of the narrow sidewalk frontage facing the Oscar-von-Miller Ring.

The Pirelli site at Bicocca, Milan, offered a situation that was more comparable to the scope of the Renault proposal. This time Meier's 'machine' took a more axial form. Nonetheless it was also broken down into courtyard blocks, open to different kinds of appropriation by the user. It was conceived not only as a park

SIEMENS OFFICE BUILDING, PERSPECTIVE OF ENTRY WITH COURT

but also a work-place, a museum and a scientific laboratory. Something of the intention of this programme-less project is revealed by the architect's description: 'To the east are located all the industrial sheds and work-places, while to the west a long park separates the modern work-space from the housing and the commercial activity that gravitates to the Viale Sarca. To the south, the scheme assumes the construction of the proposed east-west highway while to the north, it anticipates a continuation, when the Pirelli Cables Division is no longer operating.'

Few industrial re-use proposals are more playful than Meier's project for the transformation of the long-since disused Fiat plant at Lingotto. This is the famous reinforced concrete flatted factory designed by engineer Matte Trucco that once played such an iconographic role in the history of Modernism. Ironically enough Meier proposed to transform this once exemplary *usine verte* into a *unité d'habitation*! Advancing his own Smith House in Darien, Connecticut, as the late Modern equivalent of Le Corbusier's bottle-rack unit, Meier proposed that the existing car ramps would be used to feed cross-over Darien type dwellings.

All these proposals for 'cities in miniature' culminate in two urban works of great conviction; the one a diminutive work and the other taking up an entire urban block. I have in mind, of course, the cultural centre for Ulm of 1986 and the City Hall and Central Library projected for The Hague in the same year. The

scale and siting of the Ulm building is an object lesson in civic deportment and Meier was presumably premiated in this competition for the way in which he elected to restrict the extent of the existing cathedral parvis. Dividing the building into a rotunda lecture hall and a rectilinear gallery, Meier exploited the existing context in order to re-articulate the surrounding streetscape and terminate a latent rotatory movement in the urban fabric. Thus, the alley of trees that runs down one side of the cathedral is checked by a cranked urban promenade, formed by a double row of sycamores. Meier was to write: 'The architecture expresses the building's public use and function through its open design. Frequent changing vistas and spatial perceptions are provided by multi-level spaces and glass walls, all of which enhance the visitor's perception of the Cathedral, the Square and the City.'

Meier's proposed town centre for The Hague is sufficiently articulated and varied in its scale as to relate to the varied scale of the context ranging from the intimate scale of the traditional housing stock to a large block recently assembled out of such diverse complexes as Rem Koolhaas' Dance Theatre, and Carol Weber's Hotel. Like Berlage's Stock Exchange, it encloses a monumental top-lit public interior, which in this instance is somewhat over-sealed. The official description of the project adequately reveals the complexity of the urban and social intention: 'Several major spaces have been created in addition to

12

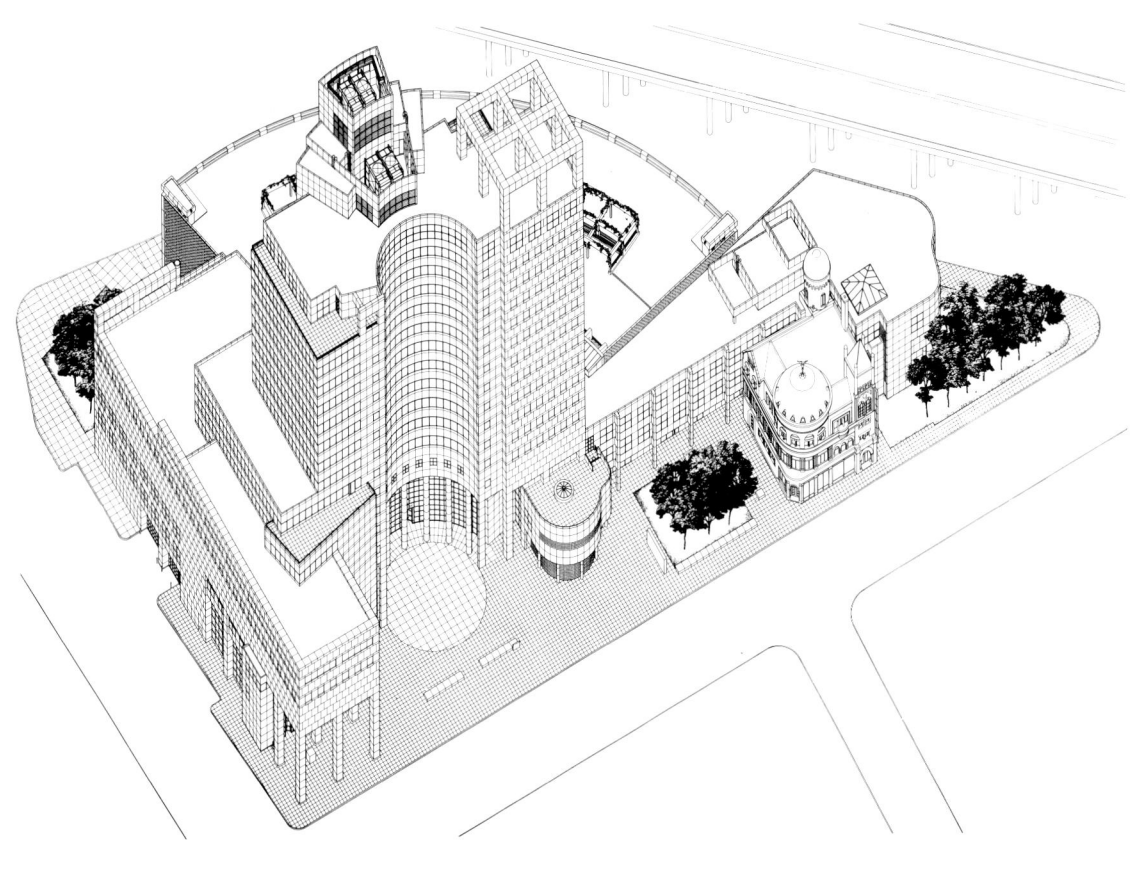

BRIDGEPORT CENTER; *OVERLEAF*: MUSEUM FÜR KUNSTHANDWERK

the new City Hall and Library; the Citizen's Hall, a wide, open atrium space within the City Hall, the entry plaza which serves as a major pedestrian focal point for the area, linking together several existing cultural institutions; and a commercial office building located at the eastern end, which functions independently of the City Hall Building. The visitor approaching the complex from the northern historic centre of the City is welcomed by the entry plaza at the northwestern corner, where one is gracefully induced to enter the City Hall by a large glass screen which breaks down the barrier between interior and exterior spaces and allows the entry plaza and the Citizen's Hall to flow together.'

Given the upper-class private patrons who have formed the main corpus of Meier's clients in the past, the last thing one would expect from this architect is a sensibility that is attuned to the problems of low-cost, urban, in-fill housing. Although this is not the first time that Meier has designed moderate-income residential stock, it is strangely paradoxical that of the 22 projects designed for Naples, in 1986, Meier's in-fill housing for the perimeter of the so-called Spanish Quarter should prove to be one of the more sensitive ideas for the redevelopment of the city. It is embarrassing that with the singular exception of Salvatore Bisogni's design for the same area, the more appropriate proposals came from outsiders rather than from Neapolitans. As Meier wrote of this, his interstitial proposal: 'Faced with the critical problem of how to put a new building in an historical context we have proposed constructing a series of housing units situated so that the existing fabric of the site is preserved. Contrary to the Corbusian vision of housing slabs isolated from their context, we have responded to the given fabric by literally extruding the building's volume from the current street plan.' Meier's ribbon housing would have acted like a suture in the urban fabric, linking an over-congested slum back into the life of the city.

It is a paradox of our cross-cultural age that Meier has found it more difficult to propose convincing urban complexes in America as his now nearly completed Bridgeport Center would suggest. Unlike José Luis Sert who had the opportunity and the capacity to leave his mark on the townscape in Cambridge, Massachusetts, Meier has yet to find a truly satisfactory approach to the partly eroded, and erratically developed, American downtown fabric. To date his Bridgeport scheme is the closest he has come to finding a formula for the insertion of massive commercial developments into the context of small-scale provincial towns. Here his strategy has been to break up the single volume required into a series of blocks of different heights and of differing syntactical affinities. However, where Sert, the European, was able to successfully graft his modern civic sensibility onto the American landscape, Meier, the American, has yet to find a suitable stempel form for the average urban grain that one

13

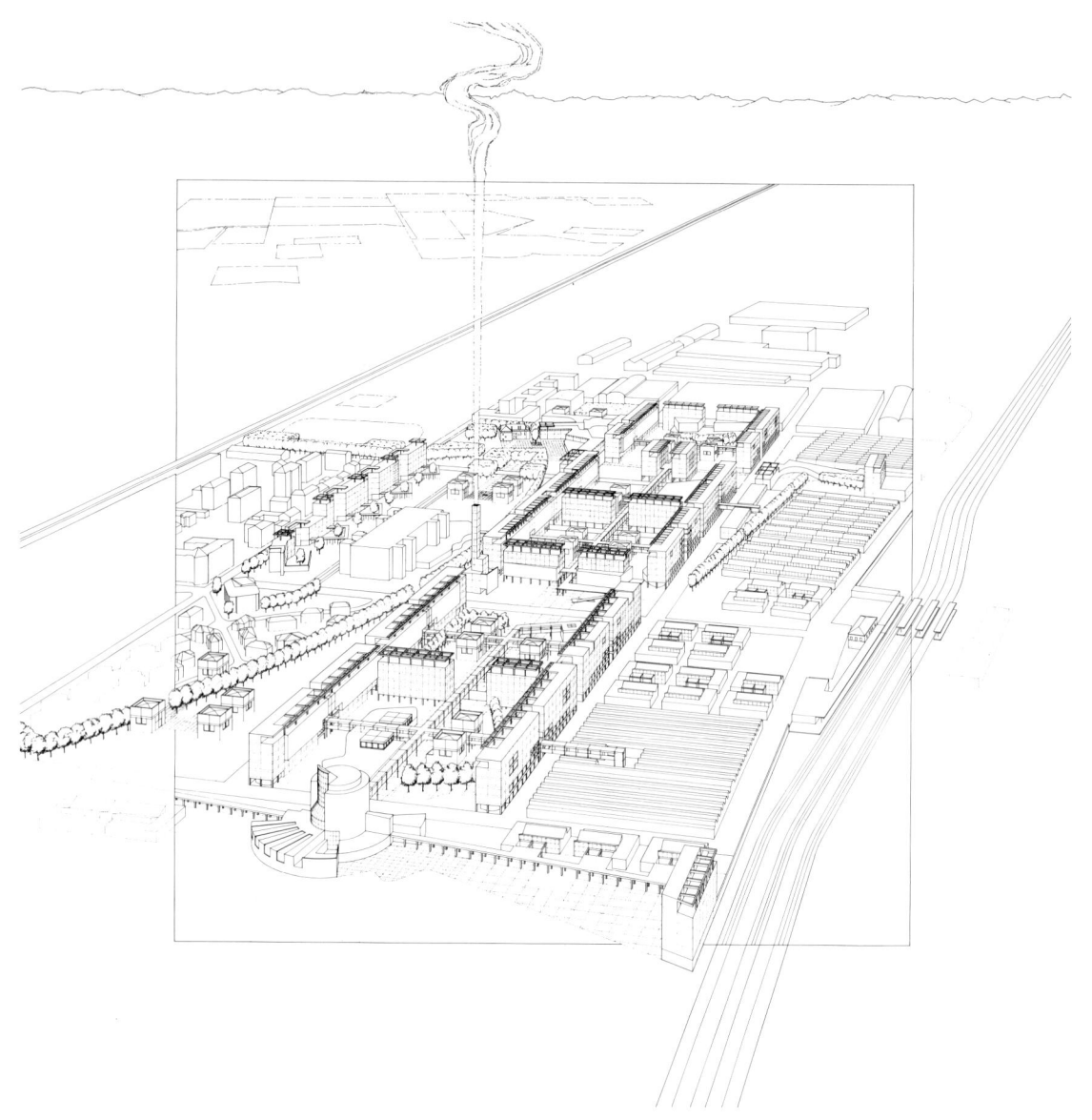

PROGETTO BICOCCA, AERIAL PERSPECTIVE

encounters in the States.

The J. Paul Getty Center, Los Angeles, promises to be Meier's ultimate city-in-miniature and not only in the USA, for it is unlikely that any other architect of this century will receive a commission of comparable grandeur. Amounting to a cultural acropolis on a 110 acre site with panoramic views over the entire Los Angeles region, the Getty Center will inevitably become a focal point within the Los Angeles megalopolis. Scheduled for completion in 1994 this foundation, carefully laid into the undulating contours of the site, will comprise of an organic clustering of complex buildings, with adjacent courts and gardens, covering some 24 acres, together with a 5 acre 'propylea' at the main entry, situated at the northern end of the site.

The main complex is organised about two converging ridges separated by a ravine. This last will be filled with earth, excavated from elsewhere in the site (the tops of the ridges, etc) and the reformed ravine will then be transformed into a terraced ornamental garden. The dominant axis running through the centre of this 'parterre', accords with the 22 1/2 degree shift in the angle of the San Diego Freeway as it travels north in a straight line from the Los Angeles County Airport. A countering secondary axis runs through the centre of the museum compound and parallels the line of the freeway before it veers eastwards away from the longitudinal body of the site. The principal public

access is from the northern entry where automobiles coming off the Sepulveda Boulevard pass under the freeway and into the propylea. Here they will be deposited in a 1,600 car, underground garage and the visitors will be then transferred to a rail-shuttle system running the three quarters of a mile and the 246 foot climb between the entrance terminus and the top of the acropolis. This shuttle will have a trip-time of five minutes and have a maximum payload of 80 passengers per trip, divided between two coupled cars. It says something for the total approach that the architect will also design the carriage work of the trams. The 700 person staff, scholars, guards, service personnel, etc, will take the Getty Drive access-road to the top of the acropolis where they will park in a subterranean undercroft below the main entry court. This court, with its three axial routes, will serve as the central distributor for the entire complex. The first of these routes conducts the visitor in a reverse direction up a monumental stair to the portico of the main 400 seat auditorium, the second leads straight up a stepped causeway into the museum and a third leads, after a short rise, into the terraced accessway of the stepped garden, to culminate in a planted amphitheatre.

In terms of mass-form the complex divides up along two ridges as follows; first, a continuous cranked sequence along the eastern ridge comprising the Auditorium and Trust Building, the Getty Conservation Institute and the Museum and second, at the

16

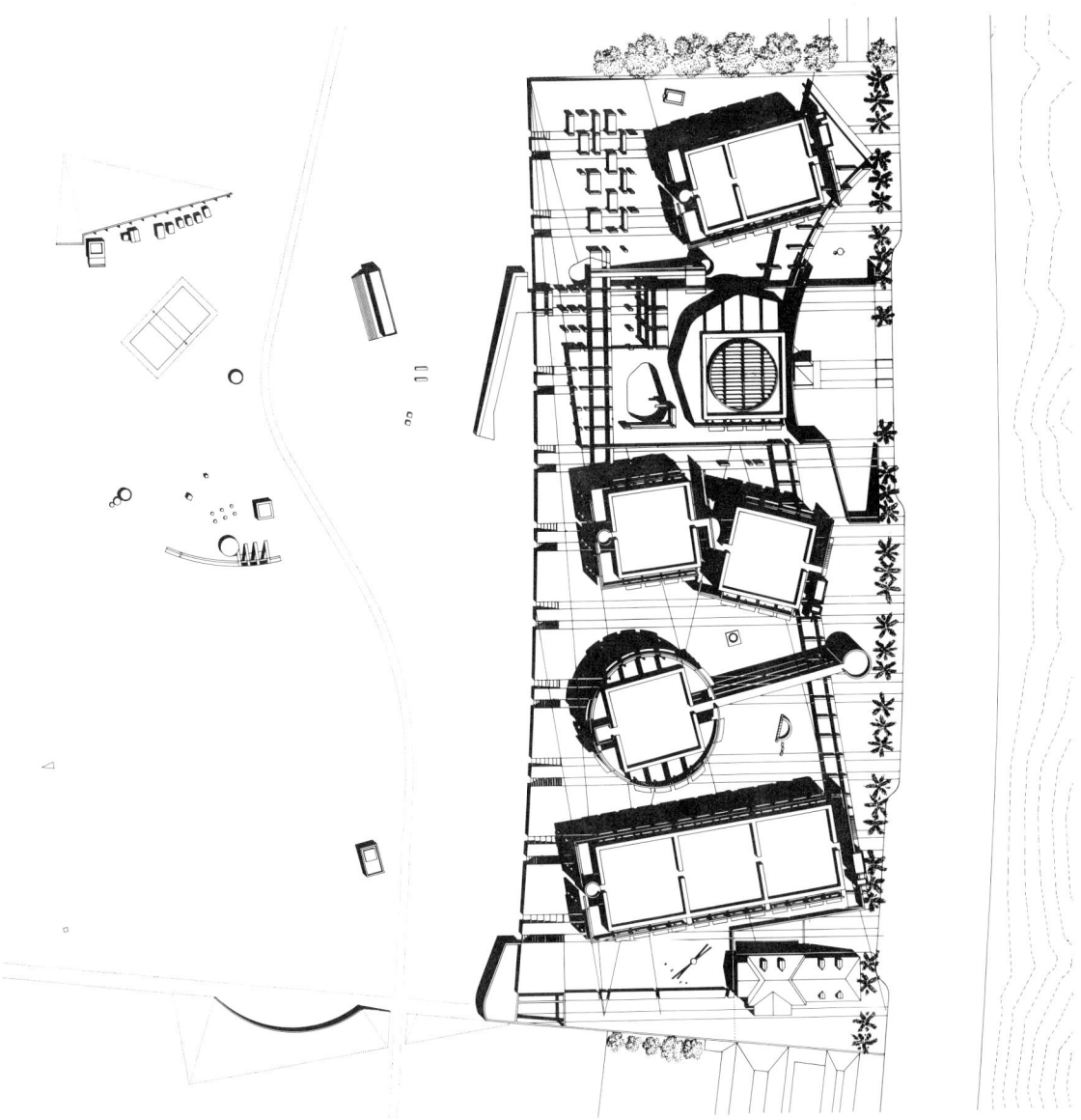

SANTA MONICA BEACH HOTEL, SITE PLAN

crest of the short western ridge, the semi-circular, Center for the History of Art and the Humanities. Between the two lies the garden and at the highest point close to the entry court, a free-standing food services building housing various restaurants and café facilities, with panoramic views, over the entire region. The most consolidated cluster of this entire assembly is appropriately enough the museum itself comprising solid-walled, top-lit prisms containing galleries, the cornices of which rise to the permitted 65 foot height above the highest point of the finished datum. The outer blank stone-faced walls of these prisms, that will be visible from the San Diego Freeway, rise some 100 feet or so above the landfall. Largely planned on an orthogonal grid, proliferating squares in plan, this complex of cubic-masses is organised in section as to allow the visitor to pass through the continuous top-lit chronological sequence of the painting collection. This is hardly the place to detail all the ancillary gallery spaces, the bookstore, the decorative arts sequence, the temporary exhibi-tion space, the photographic gallery, etc, that are woven under and even between the two top floors of the museum complex devoted to painting and sculpture. Suffice it to state, that here Meier has finally designed a museum as a public gallery and not as some kind of enlarged house. Aside from the forebuildings, housing and main auditorium, the executive offices and the conservation centre, the other primary mass-form is the Center

for the History of Art and the Humanities, situated, as it were, on the opposing ridge. This complex is organised around a top-lit centroid that penetrates the irregular iceberg of archives beneath. The central part of this vast, two-storey undercroft, housing nearly 1,000,000 volumes, together with its three-storey, 'crown' of scholars' offices, seminar rooms, plus a 200 seat lecture hall, are all concentrically organised as circumferential volumes, subdivided by partitions that radiate out from the centre.

The potential civility of this 'hill-town villa' derives as one would expect not so much from the volumetric sequences within the buildings as from the open space between them and in the three years since Meier received the commission, almost as much time has been lavished on the park-like, garden setting as on the organisation and accommodation of a demanding programme. Playing a central role in unifying this entire complex is the garden sequence that runs from the entry court, up the 'stramps' and then down through a pergola-covered descent to the penultimate framing screen, (part wall, part stoa) that is the final prelude to the amphitheatre. This straight promenade breaks up into fugal sequences to either side, animated like a modern Villa d'Este, with a primary cross-axis of water courses, interrupted by discrete basins, linking the outriding lower podium of the Art History block to the southern end of the museum court. At every successive level, as it descends, the garden breaks up laterally

17

THE HIGH MUSEUM OF ART

into a series of sub-episodes. Thus it starts with a pergola-covered 'bridgehead' extending to the Art History block, then moves down and across to connect to the lower public-datum of the museum podium and hence to the foyer of its lecture hall and so on down the site.

From a strictly architectonic point of view it could be claimed that this is Meier at his most 'baroque', where the principal of collage risks between being carried to excess and being brought to a point where one can no longer establish a field reference for each autonomous form. And while one may argue that this is the inescapable sensibility of our fragmented age, and point to the mode of 'deconstruction' running like a phantom through these exfoliating forms, one can also easily arrive at a moment where legibility disintegrates, where figures lose their reciprocal focus, where interest flags and the object, stripped of its catharsis, dissolves. In this state, the over-stimulated subject sinks into a state of distraction, so that Eliot's 'distracted from distraction by distraction' becomes the final nemesis in which architecture consumes itself.

This is the danger of which Meier is only too aware of and he knows, as he moves from the schematics stage, that everything will now depend on how well these multiple works can be profiled, proportioned, fenestrated and clad in different materials in such a way as to sharpen the figure against the ground and to resolve each into an institutional entity. Subtle topographic inflections, ambiguities, the picturesque, the lyrical, et arcadia ego of contrapuntal form and material richness, will hardly be lacking here but the ineffable qualities of presence and emptiness, these touchstones of the real in terms of a direct aesthetic experience, these are the attributes that will have to be fought for as the work unfolds. As Michael Benedickt has recently written: 'An object or building with presence has a shine, a sensuousness, a symmetry to it. Well constructed . . . every material and texture is fully itself and revealed. From the frame of the eaves of a Chinese temple to the chain that drips pearls of rain, from the brilliant colours of the Parthenon to its subtly coloured steps in the sun, enhancements of every kind have been devised . . . all in the service of presence.' (and then later) 'For architecture, emptiness implies that a building ought not to be slave to its programme, trusting and turning to accommodate our every movement . . . but rather should be formed according to innate principles of order, structure, shelter . . . and accident . . .

WESTCHESTER HOUSE

Emptiness is more akin to the idea of space, or interval. The Japanese have the word *ma* which comes close to the meaning of emptiness intended here. *Ma* is in the gaps between the stepping stones, in the silence between the notes of music, in what is made when a door slides open . . . At the Salk, the pearlescent place with its central water course and radiant tensile openness draws together the sea just beyond the hills and the sky overhead . . .'

Standing at the end of a fairly long, if sporadic line, of American cultural Utopias – Hollyhock, Taliesin, Cranbrook, Black Mountain and all the many remarkable universities and retreats of the United States the Getty Center will emerge, at its completion, in 1994, not only as a singular focus within the Los Angeles basin, but also as one of the ultimate centres of advanced cultural study in the world. And despite the 'inaccessibility' of its elite status, it will also play a major and possibly underestimated role as a public meeting place. For while the provision of a prestige helicopter pad is only too prescient, given the way that this institution will function on a global scale, it is to be wondered whether the client has yet come to terms with the inevitable popular appeal of this citadel looking over the vast panorama of the Los Angeles basin. Certainly this is a repository of world culture to be savoured at will and according to one's capacity, but have the trustees really realised the extent to which they will all come, these members of the great American public, at the rate of two thousand a day, or even more, as the museum is the last refuge of the spiritual in this, our destitute time? Where will they all go then as they flood the gardens? Where will they refresh themselves? Where will they dissipate within this enormous but as yet insufficiently articulated 80 acre wilderness park? Certainly these issues must have been raised countless times but we still have reason to raise them again, for if, as the chances are, they have been deemed to be imponderable, then nonetheless, a critic and an architect still has to ask the client, whether sufficient contingency plans have been laid. For the challenge of the city-in-miniature lies here: how do we provide a res publica and still maintain sufficient space and tranquillity for the cultivation of culture? And while this question is couched here in metaphorical terms it is nonetheless real for that.

Richard Meier – Buildings and Projects, 1979-1989, Academy Editions, London and St. Martin's Press, New York, 1990.

CHARLES JENCKS
THE RESURRECTION AND DEATH OF THE NEW MODERNS

How could the New Modernism live such a short time that tonight we announce both its birth and possible extinction? This paradox has its serious side, which can only be explained by a historical digression to thirteen years ago, the point when Modern architecture was declared non-human, but positively so.

Up until 1977, Modern architects considered themselves humanists and idealists. Modern philosophers and writers such as Nietzsche, D.H. Lawrence and Jean-Paul Sartre might have been nihilists and pessimists – with little belief in the Modern world beyond contempt – but Modern architects such as Le Corbusier, Buckminster Fuller and Walter Gropius believed in a new world of progress, science and industrialisation because they had to: architects must construct the future and, by professional ideology, believe in it passionately, or else they cannot convince clients of their dreams.

They all assumed Modern architecture would liberate mankind, would in Fuller's words, 'do more with less' material and energy, and make the world a more humane place. Of course there were always doubters around, such as Prince Charles, who reversed their equations – as he did in 1987 by saying traditional architecture was 'human' and Modern 'inhuman' – but these sceptics were a silent majority for fifty years as Modernism reigned supreme in the academies and on the street.

Then, Post-Modernism struck in the 1960s and 1970s, Modern buildings started to be blown up in 1972 and soon the fashion for this form of deconstruction became world-wide. Modern architecture was seen to fail fifteen years before the Prince called it 'inhuman', because it did not provide a sense of place, ownership, symbolism, urban identity – in short, because it was experienced as inhuman. Why was this? Why, given the fact that Le Corbusier and virtually every other architect reiterated their humanist intentions? Was this simply another Modernist ideology, like Communism in the 1930s and 1940s? Or was it a failure of theory, an inability to see how abstraction, mass production and progress for the bourgeoisie were destructive to local cultures?

It was undeniable that in almost every case, the very people for whom modern housing was intended hated and vandalised it. The deep reason, as Marshall Berman has so cogently argued, was that cultural Modernism was based on industrial *modernisation*: modernisation and progress place technology and economy above local culture, the imperatives of efficiency and profit above sentiment, and that leads directly to alienation. As Berman argued in his book, *All That is Solid Melts into Air*, and Goethe long ago showed with the quintessential Modern character Faust, the 'tragedy of development' is that in order to liberate mankind you must uproot it – deracinate it. The architect, planner and developer must tear down and destroy old patterns of life in order to create the new and improved.

It's only a slight exaggeration to compare this situation to the often quoted words of an American Air Force general in Vietnam: 'We must bomb the village in order to save it'. Such words overstate, but nonetheless suggest, the 'tragedy of development' and it has taken a long time – Berman's book was not published until 1982 – for Modernists to understand this ambivalent truth.

But I gave the date of 1977 as the point when some Modern architects no longer considered themselves idealists and humanists, because this was the year *Peter Eisenman* wrote his editorial on 'Post-Functionalism' in *Oppositions* and with it declared a New Modernism that was anti-humanist: one that displaces 'man away from the centre of his world', one which negates the idea of authorship and function and puts in their place an 'atemporal, decompositional' approach. In short, Deconstruction hit architecture, as it had literature six years before, and from that point a New Modernism was born, one that was radically abstract and consciously alienated from everyday life – the equivalent of Schoenberg's atonal music, Mallarme's pure poetry, and Mondrian's abstract painting. It's true that previously Miesian architecture stemmed from these sources, and so all the blank, minimalist curtain walls of the 1960s were, in this sense, anti-humanist, out of human scale and opposed to anthropomorphism. But the Old Modernists could not quite admit this, either to themselves or to their public. Le Corbusier, for instance, dimensioned his architecture to the Modular Man, and his anthropomorphic traces could occasionally be found in the legs of his buildings: but the other Modernists did not care much, either about empathy nor the image of the human body.

It took Peter Eisenman to proclaim the anti-humanism inherent within the Modern project and then to design a series of Deconstructionist buildings based on this new philosophy. Hence his decentered houses which do not allow the inhabitant to live in or occupy the centre; hence the Guardiola House which is perched above a spectacular view of the sea, but doesn't allow you to see it from inside because the theory of the wall placement will not permit it; hence the glass floor of House VI that divides the marital bed, or the glass floor of House X on which one cannot walk. Such architecture which is post-functional and will not tolerate human use or pleasure at some points because of its metaphysical commitment to a decentered universe, is at once very amusing for the critics, sometimes unhappy for the client and deadly serious for Eisenman. It symbolises a universe bereft of purpose, in which mankind is accidental, alienated, or architecturally 'not at home'.

This is the universe which philosophers such as Nietzsche, Sartre and Russell have been telling us now for two hundred years, is our eternal fate.

In Russell's rather melodramatic words from *A Free Man's Worship* (1914), we hear the typical nihilism of the Modern world view: 'That Man is the product of causes which had no prevision of the end they were achieving; that his origin, his growth, his hopes and fears, his loves and beliefs, are but the outcome of accidental collocations of atoms . . . that all the labours of the ages, all the devotion, all the inspiration, all the noon-day brightness of human genius, are destined to extinction in the vast death of the solar system . . . all these things, if not quite beyond dispute, are yet so nearly certain, that no philosophy which rejects them can hope to stand'.

This grim metaphysical message – the Darwinian world picture – created a nihilist movement, particularly in Moscow and Paris in the nineteenth century as the novels of Turgenev portrayed and, as Eisenman's work at the Wexner Center in Ohio shows, it can today create a very profound Deconstructionist collage. Positive Nihilism – to personify his philosophy – here slices through two existing buildings, smashes down their corners and reassembles the fragments elsewhere. It resurrects a nineteenth-century armoury not for use, not for any purpose other than to remind you it was destroyed fifty years ago, a fact which is driven in by the cuts and slashes. It surmounts one grid of building with a useless white box 'cornice'; this only has a visual function of marking a conceptual grid of 96 feet a multiple of the many other grids. This 'gridism' is quite beautiful and dazzling, but Positive Nihilism denies aesthetic intention. Post-Functional? Antihumanist? Sensual and moving? Decorative and symbolic? Yes, all of that – but only to the elite, such as you and me, who can decode these subtle texts.

The gratuitous white scaffolding (which shields no one from the sun or rain, and leads nowhere) and the frenzy of superimposed grids in the main exhibition space grids of glaring light which do not allow paintings actively subvert, if they do not destroy, the traditional museum. Eisenman says paintings which have to hang on a wall should be sent elsewhere.

All of this is provocative, creative, sensual if not 'aesthetic'; above all it's 'new' to Modernism. And, of course, it is just the tip of the iceberg, the most notable (and over-published) exemplar of the New Modernism, a tradition which has become a fashion and a fashion which has now become a flood. Every student from Hong Kong to Buenos Aires is churning out the Decon formulae and, however much Eisenman denies it, or protests that he is not the Pope of this new Establishment, these followers are mass-producing his kind of 'violated perfection'. It has many of the stylistic hallmarks which I have summarised in a diagram of Neo-Modern practice: 'self-contradictory, weaving structures', 'disjunctive complexity', 'explosive space with tilted floors', 'cocktail sticks', 'warp distortions', 'anamorphism', 'extreme abstraction', 'alien' architecture, 'frenzied cacophony', 'Degree Zero aesthetic' and so on. We all know this Neo-Modern aesthetic, perhaps too well, because it has been featured in every architectural magazine over the last two years.

This extreme fashionability has created a mood, a consensus, an *audience* – which is why you are wondering where it is going, what it adds up to, what it means. One point is clear and it was discovered by the 'First' Modernists of the late eighteenth century: the concept 'make the world anew' or the injunction 'make art new', led to a sociological truth which Wordsworth discovered: 'Every new poet must create the audience by which he is judged'. Therefore, since every Modern Movement – and there have been 25 since 1800 – seeks to 'make it new', to create a 'shock of the new', must also perforce create a new audience, or taste culture. This had another unintended consequence: if an artist like Picasso, or Duchamp, or an architect like Le Corbusier or Philip Johnson wanted to keep up with fashion and a changing audience, then he had to change style every twenty years, if not more often. To keep his cutting edge sharp Le Corbusier would even fire his assistants and clear out his firm every seven years. Today, of course, in the Post-Modern information world, the generations have sped up and been consumed by fashion every three or four years (almost approaching Andy Warhol's 'fashion limit' of fifteen minutes).

This voracious appetite for the 'new' probably sounds destructive and deconstructive of culture; and so it is. And Modernists, from 1800 onwards, have feared and on occasion attacked the fickle tyranny of fashion. So there is contradictory ideology within the Modern Movements which is at once in favour of and against constant change. Le Corbusier and the Futurists who built permanent monuments for transitory functions, indestructible concrete monoliths for a throw-away culture,

show this contradiction most clearly. However, a new group of critics and theorists have emerged since the 1970s, writers such as Marshall Berman and the Marxist David Harvey, who have shown the fatal connections between modernisation, fashion and cultural Modernism. One does not have to be a Marxist to understand that production and consumption cycles are directly related to advertisement, conspicuous consumption, the rise of the bourgeoisie and quick obsolescence – in short, fashion.

'Make it new' of the Romantics has become 'Make it different' of the Saatchis. The economy demands it, the turnover of production demands it, your and my 'aesthetic fatigue' demand it and, perhaps most importantly, the quick, competitive innovations in technology demand it.

As the fast-moving 'product cycles' of the South Koreans and Japanese show us – where the record player is replaced by the tape deck, the tape deck by the CD and the CD, in its third generation, by I can't remember what in the information world you leap generations or ossify. 'Innovate or die' is the epigram of those on the Modernist treadmill – constant innovation.

Thus you may guess some of the most vital New Modernism comes from the Japanese, and not just the youth who are so quick at taking up foreign styles, but also the older, wiser generation of Fumihiko Maki and Kazuo Shinohara. These architects in their sixties have been subject to the extreme pressures of mechanisation and Westernization for thirty years; they now feel these forces in their bones and have produced the cool, abstract silver aesthetic which they find most appropriate to constant city change. Personally, I find Fumihiko Maki's work the most satisfying and challenging of all the New Moderns in one respect. He has understood the critique of Post-Modernists and produced a small-scaled, well-detailed, high-tech architecture that is flexible rather than rigid, full of expression and variation rather than repetitive. He has humanised Modernism because he always employs five or six architects who live continuously on the site, making detailed, expressive decisions at the *last* moment. This, a result of the small-tool revolution and Japanese production, really is the *New* in New Modernism – it is acceptable innovation.

Kazuo Shinohara also creates hand-crafted high-tech, but bases his poetics of architecture on the random noise and mechanistic jungle that is apparent in all urban areas today: the road signs, electrical cables, silver trains, planes and vehicles that slide, crash or hoot about us from seven in the morning till eleven at night (much longer in Tokyo). He, like a Futurist, wants to capture this restless dynamism in his flying beams and perforated metal, his abstract grey, white and black buildings.

Why do the Neo-Moderns avoid colour? Why do they abjure polychromy and all the subtle earth colours, and attack comprehensible imagery as pastiche? A psycho-historian might say they are playing the *old* Modernist game of exclusive politics: exclude tradition, local culture, the past in order to produce what is left-over: i.e. the Minimalist means of expression. Then your audience, like a good political party, will know what you are against. A.W. Pugin who started this either/or politics in 1840 with his set of *Contrasts* was clearly against pagan Classicism and in favour of the religious Gothic; every Modernist has followed this two-slide logic and been clearly against Beaux-Arts formalism while usually in favour of White Minimalism, while today, Richard Rogers and Max Hutchinson are clearly against Prince Charles and Traditional architecture, and in favour of polychromatic pipes. I simplify the contrasts even more than they do to bring out the underlying politics of exclusion – and its elitism. It has a ruthless logic which leads inexorably to minimalism, to 'less is more' and to 'much more less is really nothing'. *Nihil est.*

But, I want to argue, there is a deeper psychological reason for

this Minimalism – one that Marshall Berman, and before him Adolf Loos and Karl Marx have begun to fathom. This explanation is likely to be resisted by Modernists of most persuasions – whether Neo or Late – precisely because it is based on the notion of psychological suppression, the necessity for the patient to deny the truth of what Dr. Marx has diagnosed. It is simply that the *creative* power of the Modernist is also the *destructive* violence of the bourgeoisie (I quote from Karl Marx's *Communist Manifesto*, which Berman calls the archetypal *Modernist manifesto*):

> 'Constant revolutionising of production, uninterrupted disturbance of all social relations, everlasting uncertainty and agitating, distinguish the bourgeois epoch from all earlier times. All fixed, fast-frozen relationships, with their train of venerable ideas and opinions, are swept away, all new-formed ones become obsolete before they can ossify. All that is solid melts into air, all that is holy is profaned, and men at last are forced to face with sober senses the real conditions of their lives and their relations with their fellow men'.

Making allowances for the sexism of this passage (most Modernists *do* speak of 'men' and 'man'), it nevertheless points to the profound truth of Modern economics, a reality which has been rediscovered again and again by economists such as Joseph Schumpeter, or multinational corporations such as Mobil Oil. The truth, and I quote from an oil advertisement of 1978, is 'Innovative Self-Destruction'. As Marx, Nietzsche, the Futurists, Le Corbusier, Marshall Berman and every Modernist since 1800 has admitted to themselves in candid moments – one must destroy to create, and particularly destroy social relationships, neighbourhoods and subcultures which have little economic power. All that is sacred will melt into air under the impact of modernisation. The ethnic neighbourhood where Marshall Berman grew up – north of New York City – was melted into air by the Modernism and highways of that great New York empire builder Robert Moses.

Perhaps no group has suffered more at the hands of destructive progress than the Jewish community, and thus today it is not only architectural or literary critics who point out this 'tragedy of development', but those who trace the destruction-machine of the Nazis directly to the *Zeitgeist* of Enlightenment rationalism – its dark side, its suppressed 'other'. Many books are appearing on these connections, but Zygmunt Bauman's title, recently published by Oxford, says it as bluntly and directly as you can: *Modernity and the Holocaust*. According to Bauman, the Holocaust was not an aberration of modern society and the ideology of Modernity, but utterly typical of them. Scientific racism and mass-produced eugenics – improving the human species by applying the rational techniques of market gardening – follow from the Modernist emphasis on rationality, efficiency and instrumental reason. The Nazis, Bauman argues, carried out the extermination of 6 million Jews by applying cool, bureaucratic logic and the latest technology to the killing process.

But, authors are now showing, the dark side of Modernity does not end here. It is argued by the German-American historian Theodore van Laue, in *The World Revolution of Westernization*, that the destructive potential of modernisation goes beyond the Holocaust. This book, which was praised by Paul Kennedy in the *TLS*, makes the radical, indeed extreme, point that Westernised modernisation is ultimately responsible for two world wars and the misery that the Second and Third Worlds now face through social upheavals in India, Pakistan, Indonesia, the Philippines, and elsewhere.

That is quite a burden for Modernists to contemplate. The Third World, unlike the West, has had to go through modernisation quickly and in the guise of Westernisation, so they suffer a double trauma: a social earthquake followed immediately by a cultural tidal-wave. First deracination in the face of economic and technological rationalisation and then cultural suicide, since Modernism is always brought in with, and as, Western culture. Traditional manners, customs, dress and values are dropped. Now the Japanese and Koreans wear the Modern two-piece suit as they churn out their foreign style motor cars, more Western than the West.

Significantly, it is often Jewish architects – such as Peter Eisenman, Daniel Libeskind and Frank Gehry – who make the most of their Jewishness *and* their Neo-Modernism (although they probably would avoid these labels). The three have written and talked about the problems of being an outsider in a dominant culture of Wasps, or Anglo-Saxons; they have built memorials to, or symbolic of, the Holocaust, and have embraced a Modernism of 'otherness' – of subversion, dissent and dislocation. The nihilism of the cosmos, or just the cynicism of everyday commercial life, is never far from their thoughts and they often represent this unthinkable otherness in their elaborate complications. So the new aesthetic of the New Modernism comes directly from the metaphysics of nihilism they share; it represents this world view or *episteme*.

But why, to return to my psycho-historical question, is their style always abstract and not accessible to the public, why are their buildings largely silver, white, black (or occasionally with Bernard Tschumi, fire-engine red – which he describes significantly as a non-colour)? Indeed, why has Modernism, which has been revised at least 25 times since 1800, always tended towards abstraction? The conclusion towards which Karl Marx, Adolf Loos and Marshall Berman inexorably lead is that Modernists come from the bourgeoisie and this middle class, being the most destructive-creative group in history, simply cannot admit that they are either bourgeois, or destructive. Bourgeois self-loathing finds its counterpart, as Tom Wolfe has argued, in the anti-bourgeois style of the Bauhaus. What unites Modern, Late and Neo-Modernists is that their abstraction, trying to be proletarian – or classless, or anti-bourgeois – is the *recurrent* style of the middle class.

As Berman says, their secret – a secret they have managed to keep even from themselves – is that, behind their facades, they are the most violently destructive ruling class in history. All the anarchic, measureless, explosive drives that a later generation will baptise by the name of 'nihilism'– drives that Nietzsche and his followers will ascribe to such cosmic traumas as the Death of God – are located by Marx in the seemingly banal everyday

working of the market economy. He unveils the modern bourgeois as consummate nihilists on a far vaster scale than modern intellectuals can conceive.

As Modernists melt ethnic neighbourhoods into air, they must suppress this fact behind an ideology of progress and a style of blank abstraction. The timeless aesthetic, the technological model of glistening silver machinery, carries no history, no culture, no tears.

It is simply the style without guilt, without a past, without connections – the acontextual style of an airplane that goes everywhere. Modernists, as we know, have always hated the bourgeoisie and tried to shock, or *epater* this class because it was at once, as Marx insisted, both the most destructive *and* the most reactionary in history. The avant-garde also loathed this class because they themselves came from and were sustained by it. Their patrons were the nouveaux-riches, and between them the avant-garde and bourgeoisie were destroying *and* creating everything in sight. Modernists unable to face this historical truth, this complicity and its suppression, return again and again to abstraction, and the Degree Zero style. It's the equivalent of a *tabula rasa*, a self-cleansing, a clearing out of the messy clutter of the past and social pluralism – the cleansing of Pontius Pilate.

The New Modernism, like the previous 25 revivals of this hardy phoenix-bird, I will predict, aspire to the condition of industrial design because that, more than any other, moves freely across national and cultural boundaries – even miraculously across time. And time, the changing spirit of time, the *Zeitgeist*, the respected yet feared beast of Modernism, is at once the demon of progress and fashion. *Haute couture* both brings in the 'new stock' and declares poignantly, as it does at the end of every year's production, that the old fashion is 'dead stock'.

'Burn what you love, love what you burn' Le Corbusier exhorted, quoting Nietzsche as he jumped from one style to the next, from Art Nouveau to Classicism to Purism to Brutalism to High Tech – and periodically fired his staff. While it is true Modernism changes slower than fashion, they both celebrate the eternal present, and corresponding loss of historical consciousness. Gore Vidal calls the US 'the United States of Amnesia' and Peter Eisenman often makes from his name the acrostic 'amnesia'. Why? Because fashion and Modernism both demand the end of memory so that we can revive the recent past without guilt, without knowing we are repeating a previous series of 'Neos'. When Pop artists revived Dada without knowing it, Marcel Duchamp snapped contemptuously, 'Neo-Dada', and when Jeff Koons revived Pop Art recently those with longer memories complained, 'Neo-Neo-Dada-Dada'. But their complaints fell on lobotomised ears, if ears can be subtracted of memory.

What about the recent history of architecture? In the late 1970s, when Post-Modernism was challenging the dominant orthodoxy of Modern architecture, I coined the term 'Late-Modern architecture' to distinguish those who had also shifted from High Modernism – Rogers, Foster, Meier – but were not interested in the Post-Modern concerns of urban context, ornament and symbolism. The designation was accepted by critics and historians *Vincent Scully, Reyner Banham, John Summerson* and even the ideologically opposed Kenneth Frampton. But some architects had trouble with the notion of 'Late' since as Modernists, they always wanted to be 'Early', or even better, 'First'. In the mid-eighties, seeing that a 'Neo-Modern' label was being applied by New York critics to Foster and Rogers, and understanding that the Deconstructionists and Eisenman were really 'new' to Modern architecture, I coined the term 'New Moderns'.

The point of this phrase was its self-conscious irony, its double newness which the phrase 'Neo-Modern' did not quite bring out. The self-conscious formulation also reflected the only thing that united this heterogeneous group: they all hated the Post-Modern, especially the classical brand. Of course there were other forces and motives: the youth wanted a 'new, improved Modernism'.

There were also a handful of architects practising a recognisable 'Neo-Constructivism'. This revival by Rem Koolhaas, Bernard Tschumi, Zaha Hadid, Frank Gehry and Coop Himmelblau was quite conscious, and so the final requisite for designating the movement was provided. Like Neo-Classicism it self-consciously revived a dead style (it was not a *survival* like Late-Modernism); it had a new philosophy, new aesthetic and some answers to the critique of Post-Modernism. Two years ago, I explained this phrase to Jonathan Glancey, who later asked me to write some articles on it for *The Independent*. Little did I know, Jonathan himself thought the label so felicitous that he began beavering away as fast as possible on a book with the same title as mine. This has recently appeared. So now we have 'The New Moderns'– 'The New Moderns', or as I would like to rephrase it, 'The New New Moderns Moderns' to bring out the ridiculous redundancy which reveals an unwelcome truth: deep in the bowels of Modernism lurks the great anxiety, and spectre, of fashion.

Whereas Gropius and the Pioneers proclaimed a heroic new Modern architecture in 1919 as a crystal symbol of new faith in socialism and communal work; whereas Le Corbusier preached *l'Esprit Nouveau* in 1920 as the new spirit of constructing mass-production houses, Glancey defines today's Pioneers just in terms of fashion, for creating a new environment free from Post-Modern clutter. His most theoretical statement is this, 'The New Moderns are those people who have begun and will increasingly choose a clean, spacious, light and clutter-free architecture in the l990s and beyond. They are Pioneers in the true sense because they have the vision and strength to jump clear over the hurdle of fake historic styles ...'

'True Pioneers' for jumping *this* hurdle ? Has Glancey forgotten that ever since Le Corbusier's self-proclaimed 'vacuum-cleaning period' of architecture, we've had a 'Spring Clean' every year? White Minimalist architecture has never stopped being built since the 1920s, it continued as an unbroken tradition.

Throughout Glancey's lusciously illustrated book one searches for definitions of the New Moderns, or theoretical, historical or cultural understanding something either the equivalent of the Modernist belief in technology or social emancipation, or Eisenman's belief in Deconstruction. But one finds only recipes, or prescriptions, and I quote again: '[The New Modern stair] is often the single most decorative device in the house' (p 41) or, 'The New Modern house is a gallery' (p. 108), or 'The New Modern kitchen is not ashamed of what it is ... a ship's galley or a domestic engine room' (p. 130), or 'The New Modern dream is having the principal window at floor level for the pleasure of lying in bed while watching the world outside' (pp. 151-153).

Of course Post-Modernists have been putting windows right next to the floor for years – I did it so I could see ants on the ground fighting – but we didn't make it to a principle of the new 'dream'. My favourite of the recipes, with its deconstructed grammar, concerns the category Glancey calls 'New Modernism at night', for here we find once again revealing echoes of that psychological truth which has to be suppressed. 'By night, New Modern children [sic] enjoy the psychological security of their houses. A house without spooky corridors and worrisome staircases is easy on a child's impressionable mind. The openness of a New Modern house takes away at least some of the stuff that nightmares are made of' (p. 93). Oh, those nightmares of New Modern children ... But they must be confused, since previously we've been shown countless ornamental staircases which are difficult to negotiate, because according to a key maxim they're supposed to be the most 'decorative device in the house'. What are we to think of these two conflicting precepts? On reflection it's clear that the first of Glancey's principles is the deciding one, that an absence of 'clutter' means those 'decorative' staircases have got to go, and stop giving New Modern children their nightmares. Thus another victory of the Degree Zero Style, of minimalism beating off ornament, complexity and history. But this time round, the ascetic message of renunciation is served up in a new way – between glossy covers with over 250 very appetizing full-colour photos – the kind of well-flavoured imagery that makes a *House and Garden* editor salivate.

How can we explain this mixed message – the *cuisine minceur* of sensory deprivation served up as a visual feast? A clue is given in the back of the book where the publisher Mitchell Beazley has helpfully provided a list of 'stores' where one can purchase these dietary pleasures – in London, Milan, Paris, Barcelona, Tokyo, New York and West Germany.

Glancey, according to the back flap, is a regular contributor to *Vogue* and *The World of Interiors*, and, I suppose, these further clues tell us about the audience for the book and its proper mode of consumption: it is not meant to be read but visually eaten, after coffee and *After Eight* along with *The English Gentlewoman's Garden, The English Gentleman's Pantry* and *The English Style*. This is the ultimate bourgeois genre, the glossy monthly or annual, in which the text is not so much an argument or theory, but a long caption about a transient way of life, to be emulated for fifteen minutes. That is the point of this long aside. The New Modernism whose birth was announced early this afternoon, is hanging by a thread this evening, victim of too much colour-separation. This could be the shortest movement in Modernist history – the Resurrection and Death – as my title would have it, between inception and commercialisation, birth and death by coffee-table.

I do not mean to be cynical about this fact, just descriptive. When Post-Modernism started as a worldwide tradition in the mid-seventies, I predicted its ageing the minute Philip Johnson made the front page of *The New York Times* with the AT&T Building in March 1978. It lasted four more years as the leading world movement, but it could not survive for long the embrace of commercial culture, any more than the 25 previous Modern movements that had succeeded, and then been distorted because of their success. Fashion and commercial success warp cultural movements into magazines as fast as technological and economic change melt neighbourhoods into air, and these grim reapers are essential to, not an aberration of, Modernity.

This can be understood from the attitudes in 1890 when tabloid journalism and magazine culture became pervasive, when the word 'Modernism' in France and Germany summarised the new consciousness of fashion. The enjoyment of constant change, the stimulation of *The Yellow Book* and next month's magazine, created both an appetite for more change and a world-weariness associated with the *fin de siecle*. This is not so different from today's mood.

Recently, I had an exchange with Philip Johnson concerning the inexorable march of fashion and its propensity to consume everything in its path:

CJ: What has happened since our talk on the Decon Show and its effects ?

PJ: The effects were as I prophesied: everybody denied the word and the concept; but then architects like Peter Pran, designer of one of the largest firms in America, creates these buildings with everything flying about everywhere.

CJ: But that's the Modernist problem. Modernism is directly related to fast-changing fashions and stylistic shifts. No sooner do you have a 'live' movement than it is turned into a fashion, to make way for the next one. This is where there is a hidden anti-creativity within the fashion industry.

PJ: I don't think that is avoidable with the present communications. What we need is a Mies van der Rohe or Le Corbusier coming up.

CJ: But they can't come because the system moves fast and precludes it. Fashion didn't smother the Twenties, did it?

PJ: Why didn't it?

CJ: Because the speed of production was slower. You said that Michael Graves didn't grow into a major Post-Modernist because of over-production. And why is Deconstruction deconstructing? It's the process of quick speed which makes everything still-born, and that's what pushes everybody on.

PJ: Except Classicism, which would be a Rock of Gibraltar in the swirling, changing world . . .

CJ: Since the sixties the situation has only deepened. You were saying, 'It's all changing, it's all fun . . .'

PJ: No rules.

CJ: You were celebrating the Nietzschean, Dionysian aspect of creativity and fashion. And you were facing its nihilistic overtones. . .

PJ: Society is eating its own children every morning for breakfast.

At which point we stopped and had lunch.

Of course, I do not expect the New Modernism to be in the morgue *tomorrow*, latest victim of the consumption industry, because the architects I have written about – Eisenman, Libeskind, Koolhaas, Morphosis, Maki and Shinohara – have too much to say and build which is authentic and really new. They will not be stopped by the voracious Saturn of Fashion devouring its young, although their message and style will, probably, soon be blunted and warped by the overexposure.

We are all subject to this quick obsolescence, to being consumed by success, just as all of us here are probably un-signed-up members of the bourgeoisie. We may not like it, we may protest and some may do their utmost to be unfashionable. But since the nineteenth century, High Culture has been digested more and more quickly by mass culture, a fact that was understood at the time by the German theoretician Adolf Goller. According to Ernst Gombrich, who told me about this idea, the notion of 'aesthetic fatigue' has been in the air and considered since then. Architects, artists, writers have known that our culture feeds on the 'new', eats as much as possible and then gets quickly satiated with the old novelty. As Oscar Wilde said, summarising the problem: 'Nothing is so dangerous as being too modern, one is apt to grow old-fashioned quite suddenly'.

Let us then, while the Neo-Modernism is still young, enjoy it for momentary pleasures and deeper insights, before it is completely known and exhausted. The 'life of forms in art' has a certain periodicity and today many of the New Moderns are at their most creative. I, like some of you, may question their philosophy, their nihilism and abstraction, and feel the fine constructional detailing of Fumihiko Maki has more to give architecture in the future than deconstructional collage: but we have to value all these architects because of their creativity and integrity whether or not we share their beliefs.

Beyond this there is the reconsideration of Modernity coming from *within* the tradition. After being criticised by Post-Modernists and Traditionalists for fifteen years, Modernists themselves are finally facing up to the negative aspects of their tradition and are reassessing their history, ideology and practice. It's a painful reassessment, especially if the fundamental problems are acknowledged. Above all of them is the recognition that modernisation and social progress have also necessarily led to the destruction of cultures and that this 'tragedy of development' is both a cross to bear and a social problem to ameliorate. After the writings of Marshall Berman and David Harvey – two Modernists whose new theories acknowledge these facts – there's no going back, no escape from seeing 'destruction/creation' cycles for what they are – the engine of the bourgeois class, fashion and our own boredom.

The renewed calls for a 'social architecture' – to which all parties lay claim (Prince Charles', the ecologists', the Post-Modernists etc.) are now made within a completely different spectrum than that of the 1920s. Since we are still living with their mistakes, with bombed out cities, architects will not easily be given the license for mass development that existed from 1945 to 1965, unless it is in such free-fire zones as the Docklands – and here it comes from the developers not the State, from economic not social motives. Instead the New Modernists, like other architects, will operate at a more piecemeal scale – countering Le Corbusier's final solution to the housing problem – with various strategies such as small-block planning and broken-up volumes that characterise Frank Gehry and Rem Koolhaas' work. Secondly, the New Modernists, such as Daniel Libeskind, will acknowledge the tenuous relationship to time, change and culture which exists deep in the project of Modernity. Speaking of his Jewish Museum for Berlin, Libeskind mentions a 'discontinuous void', the 'voided void' in the middle of the scheme which is worn as an emblem, something that makes the absence of the 200,000 Berlin Jews a represented presence; also he alludes to 200 years of Berlin Baroque architecture. So, unlike Old-Modernism, his abstractions are culture and time sensitive. Like Post-Modernists and Eisenman's work, he symbolises the past, present and future, although without an easily accessible code.

To summarise then is the emergent paradigm: with the writings of Berman and Harvey and the architecture of Eisenman, Maki, Gehry and Libeskind, there is a new living Modernism which has learned to overcome – or at least acknowledge – the horrific lessons of the Old Modernism. It's a painful process, for those still committed to the movement, but as Oscar Wilde also said: 'experience is the name we give to our mistakes'. We have a lot of experience yet to come.

OSAKA FOLLY

DANIEL LIBESKIND
BETWEEN THE LINES

I did not come to speak about my building but about the New Modernism, as it has been called. I would like to illustrate a process of thought and a confrontation with certain issues. It is clear that the end of the 20th century is not the end of a walkway, despite that apocalyptic feeling that the year 2000 and tremendous changes will come to us very soon. There is a feeling that something has happened culturally, across the barriers of old that has fundamentally altered the mood and modality of people's feelings, desires, and consequently, thoughts. I think that what has changed is the realisation that Modernity was not a period of 10, 20 or 100 years, but that Modernity has been a period of about 3000 years and it is now coming to an end. I mean the period of enlightened human intellect with reality, that great Socratic and pre-Socratic contribution to seeing the world is coming to an end. It will still go on for thousands of years, but in the spiritual sense one has already seen an empirical reality, an absolute end to a particular mode of a relationship to the world. That mode I would have called the mode of reasonable human response to an unreasonable absurdity of the cosmic situation. Of course all of the Classic philosophers have always started with the fact that human existence is absurd, (there's no good thinker that didn't start with that thought). The purpose of life is seemingly not to live, the purpose of life seems to be death for the Modern agnostic thinkers, such as Heidegger and Millaponte. Being towards death even entered a cliché in the everyday vocabulary. After Auswitz and Hiroshima, things will no longer be the same, not because we cannot rebuild the world in a better way, but because certain experiences and the capacity of certain experiences comes to an end.

I was fortunate to participate in a competition in the city of Berlin, of which over 50 percent had been destroyed during World War Two. One out of every two buildings was destroyed and the rest are on shaky ground. The competition was a very interesting one because it ties the question of Modernity with the resources of the human spirit by committing itself to a project called 'Extension of the Berlin Museum with the Jewish Museum Department'. It is an incredible concept; I thought about it for a long time. How can one extend the history of Berlin with the history of that very absoluteness, that very absolute ending of the

history which is implicated in the so-called 'Jewish question'; in the actual physical absence of a Jewish community in Berlin? Of course there are some that have come back, but from the 200 thousand people in the Jewish community, which was a very famous and resourceful one, to 2,000 immigrants from the Soviet Union, one cannot say that we see a reconcilable realm here. In some sense, the New Modernity is an end, a certain kind of end. It is not necessarily an endgame, as in Super Modernism or New Modernism in the Godot or Beckett-like way, but it is an end. As an architect, I and many of my colleagues and others in different disciplines enter a realm which is not very clear, it is not a realm of reasons, it is not a realm of clearly laid out categories, it is a deeply ambiguous realm because not much is seen in it, not much horizon, not much openness. I do not care about reunification, the World Bank, or the fact that Coca Cola is the number one name recognised by people all over the world, because I think the human being is a much more capable being than has been credited, especially by Western historians who are mostly men. Entering the end I think also means entering the implications of all the resources that have been brought together to the end, and in this museum project what has been brought to an end is, number one, the history of Berlin, number two, the history of the Jewish community as they existed traditionally in Europe and number three the test of architecture, to be able to programmatically and socially deal with the end – not as a scenario but as a condition. I think it was Franz Kafka who said that great writers begin to work after their death. While they are alive we do not know who the great writers are because they are all writing, but he said that the minute they die we know who the great writers are because then they begin to really write. He was right; we are still getting letters from Kafka, and they are not the letters that he wrote to his father and his friends. When Jesus was crucified, his disciples thought that the world was going to end the next day, or if not that day then the day after, or three or four days later or maybe next week. By the time St. Augustine arrived at the City of God, we had been waiting for 500 years and the world still had not come to an end. The world is growing old, he said, and we must become modern to deal with it. I think 'Modernus' was first used by St. Augustine in the context of a confrontation with an

end which is not ending.

I would like to read this short statement about this project, the Berlin Museum extended by the Jewish Museum. The official name of the project is 'The Extension of the Berlin Museum with the Jewish Museum' but I have called it 'Between the Lines'. I call it this because it is a project about two lines of thinking, organisation and relationship. One is a straight line, but broken into many fragments: the other is a tortuous line, but continuing infinitely. These two lines develop architecturally and programmatically through a limited but definite dialogue. They also fall apart, become disengaged, and are seen as separated. In this way, they expose a void that runs through architecture and through this museum – a discontinuous void. And in turn, this discontinuous void materialises itself in the continuous space outside as something that has been ruined, or rather as the solid residue of an independent structure; what I call the voided void. Then there is a fragmentation and splintering, marking the lack of coherence of the museum as a whole, showing that it has come undone in order to become accessible, both functionally and intellectually.

The site is the centre of the old city Berlin on Lindenstrasse near the famous baroque intersection of Wilhelmstrasse, Friedrichstrasse and Lindenstrasse. I felt that the physical trace of Berlin was not the only trace, but rather that there was an invisible matrix or anamnesis of connections in relationship. I found this connection between figures of Germans and Jews; between the particular history of Berlin, and between the Jewish history of Germany and of Berlin. I felt that certain people (who carried a certain spirit, that is why they were exterminated, as physical beings who carried a certain spirit) and particularly certain writers, people in music, art and poetry, formed the link between Jewish culture and German culture. So I found this connection and I plotted an irrational matrix which was in the form of a system of squared triangles which would yield some reference to the emblematics of a distorted star of David: the yellow star that was so frequently worn on the site. This distorted matrix is imploded into the form of the museum; it is not as kitsch as having the star on an invisible set of streets, it is the projection of that star into the linear geometrics of the museum, and that is why the museum is a crazy looking form. I looked for addresses of where these people lived or where they worked, for example someone like Rachel Varnhagen, a very famous literary lady who single handedly created the German Literary cult, I connected with Friedrich Schleiermacher, the theologian who is buried immediately next to her, and Paul Célan, the poet, to someone like Mies van der Rohe. I was quite surprised that it was not so difficult to hear the address that these people made, to the City, and it was not difficult to find the emblem of their address in the very lineaments of a non-monumental structure: that they formed a particular urban and cultural constellation of Universal History.

Another aspect of the project was Arnold Schönberg. I was always interested in the music of Schönberg and in particular his period in Berlin, before he got kicked out of the Academy. His greatest work is an opera called *Moses and Aaron* which he could not complete. For some reason, the logic of the text, which was the relationship between Moses and Aaron, between, you can say, the revealed and unimaginable truth and the spoken and mass-produced people's truth, lead to an impasse in which the music and the text written by Schönberg could not be completed. It is an incomplete form when it is performed. In the end, Moses does not sing, he just speaks 'oh word, thou word' and you can understand it actually as a text as opposed to the norm of opera whose performance usually obliterates the text. So it is the only opera which I can understand. When there is singing you cannot understand the words, but when there is no more singing, you can understand very well the missing word uttered by Moses, which is the call for the word. That was the second aspect.

I was interested in the names of those people, mainly Jews, who were deported from Berlin from 1933 onwards, during the fatal years that one knows historically. I received from Bonn two very large volumes, thicker than a telephone book, called 'Gedenkbuch' they are incredibly impressive because all they contain are names, just names, dates of birth, dates of deportation and presumed places where these people were murdered. So, I looked for the names, that I was familiar with, for my own interest, firstly, and secondly out of my interest. I looked up the name Berlin, and I was not surprised to find pages and pages of Berliners; they wound up in Lodz or Riga or some other place far from Berlin, in concentration camps. This was the third aspect of this three-dimensional structure of the project.

The fourth aspect was the one text that I was familiar with, and have always appreciated, about the modern city, called *One Way Street* by Walter Benjamin, which is a walk to the end, a walk along a one-way street that comes to an end.

The first one was the invisible and irrationally connected star which shines with absent light of individual address. The second one is the cut of Act Two of *Moses and Aaron* which has to do with the non-musical fulfilment of the word, the third aspect is that of the deported or missing Berliners, and the fourth aspect was the one-way street aspect of the City.

In specific terms, its a large building, 10,000 square metres, budgeted initially for 77 million deutschemarks, but I think it would cost more because I propose to re-establish the staircase in the old Baroque building which is part of the museum. The extension is cut through the building, goes under, crisscrosses underground and materialises itself independently on the outside, but dependently vis-á-vis the interior of the old Baroque building. The fragmentation within the scheme is a kind of spacing or separation brought about by the history of Berlin, a phenomenon which can only be experienced as the effect of time, and at the same time as the temporal fulfilment of what is no longer there. And out of this absolute event of history which is nothing other than the Holocaust with its concentration camps, annihilation and complete burn-out of meaningful development of the city, and of humanity – out of this event which shatters this place comes a gift of that which cannot really be given by architecture. Namely a preservation of the offering, a guardian night watch, as I call it, over absent and future possible meaning. So that, out of the disaster of what was too late, comes what is early and, out of what is very distant, comes what is very close. I said it was an absolute event, because that is one aspect which is very important to think about – after those survivors of the Holocaust, no one can die. If one has not been a survivor, in that sense, we are now doomed to be survivors, which means that our relationship to death has also been transformed, by technology, development and progress.

The work is conceived as a museum for all Berliners, for all citizens. Not only those of the present, but those of the future and the past who should find their heritage and hope in this particular place, which is to transcend involvement and become participation. With its special emphasis on housing the Jewish Museum, it is an attempt to give a voice to a common fate – to the contradictions of the ordered and disordered, the chosen and not chosen, the vocal and silent. In this sense, the particular urban condition of Lindenstrasse, of this area of the city, becomes the spiritual site, the nexus, where Berlin's precarious destiny is mirrored, fractured and displaced – but also transformed and transgressed. The past fatality of the German/Jewish cultural relation in Berlin is enacted now in the realm of the invisible. It is this invisibility which I have tried to bring to visibility.

So the new extension is conceived as an emblem, where the

invisible, the void, makes itself apparent as such. The void and the invisible are the structural features that have been gathered in the space of Berlin and exposed in an architecture in which the unnamed remains because the names keep still. The existing building is tied to the extension underground, preserving the contradictory autonomy of both the old building and the new building on the surface, while binding the two together in depth, underground.

The museum, which is very difficult to measure because of its fragmentation, exists in the relationship between the two architectures and two forms, which are not reciprocal. Thus one gets the urban, architectural and functional paradox of the closed-open, stable-unstable, classical-modern, museum-amusement. This process is no longer reconcilable with some theoretical utopia and no longer presupposes the fictitious stability of state, power or organisation, but, in contrast, presupposes what does not change; and what does not change in my view is change preceding directly out of that which would exclude changing attitudes and unchanging opinions alike.

In terms of the city, the idea is to give a new value to the existing context, by transforming the urban field into an open, and what I would call a hope-oriented matrix. The proposed expansion, therefore, is characterised by a series of real and implied transformations of the site, which go beyond the existing forms of the site and of architecture. The compactness of the traditional street pattern is gradually dissolved from its Baroque origins and then related diagonally to the housing schemes of the 60s and the new IBA project of the 70s.

The new structure then, through a series of contrasts, engages the existing housing blocks and public structures in a totally new dialogue, creating an intense field. In terms of the organisation of the building and the required functions, the extension provides the Berlin Museum with an entire set of new and different spaces, which act, again, as an exchange between a narrative and non-narrative aspect. In other words, the museum is a zigzag with a structural rib, which is the void of the Jewish Museum running across it. This void is something which every participant in the museum will experience as his or her absent presence.

On the other hand, the void has been extracted out of the building, cut out surgically, rotated in the site and materialised in terms of fragments or shards that have no access from the public level, but are accessible only underground and in very special ways. Therefore, standard exhibition rooms and traditional public spaces have also been re-thought and distributed in a myriad of complex trajectories – on, above and underground – and those trajectories gradually and systematically transform themselves in their form, function and significance. In other words, it is really not a museum which involves the spectator – it is a museum which seeks to alienate the viewer who is after the history of Berlin. By alienation, the viewer is given a distance in order to see what the horizon of Modernity looks like, it is not simply blank.

That is basically a summary of how the building works. It is not a collage, a collision or a dialectic, but a new type of organization which is organized around the void, around what is not visible. And what is not visible is the collection of this Jewish Museum, which is reducible to archival material, since its physicality has disappeared. The problem of the Jewish Museum is taken also as the problem of the Jewish culture itself – as the problem of an avant-garde of humanity; an avant-garde that has been incinerated in its own history, in the Holocaust. In this sense, I believe this scheme joins architecture to questions that are now relevant to all humanity. What I have tried to say is that the Jewish history of Berlin is not separated from the history of Modernity, from the destiny of this incineration of history; they are bound together. But bound not through any obvious forms, but rather through a negativity; through a negativity, an absence of meanings and an absence of objects. Absence, therefore, serves as a way of binding in depth, and in a totally different manner, the shared hopes of people. It is a conception which is absolutely opposed to reducing architecture to a detached memorial or to a memorial detachment.

JEWISH EXTENSION TO THE BERLIN MUSEUM, PLAN OF THE URBAN SCALE WITH THE INVISIBLE ACCESS

TATE GALLERY DISCUSSION

I would like to ask the panel to respond to the question about colour, why deny yourselves the use of colour?

Richard Meier: Having taught for a long time and gone to various schools of architecture, no matter what I say or do the first question is always, 'Why are the buildings white?' The answer that I have failed to convey, both through what I've said and through the images themselves, is why they are white, why the reading of the planes is clearer when it is white as opposed to painting it some other colour that would make it recede. The relationship between linear and planar elements is important to me and is perhaps best expressed in their whiteness. The buildings are not white, they are many colours by the relationship to their situation, by the way in which the sun changes from the morning to the evening, by the way the colour changes from summer to autumn and how the buildings also change in response to the way in which they are perceived.

Colin Stansfield Smith: *I've always had an understanding, particularly in this area of Western Europe, that Modernism had an association with a social purpose. What worries me is that the social cause of Modernism does not seem to get a mention here.*

Charles Jencks: I certainly mentioned its absence. My point was that The New Moderns do not believe in enlightenment progress nor the social anymore. They do not think it's possible anymore, the way that they did in the 20s. And that is one of the things that make them 'New'; they want to have Modernism without the social agenda.

Richard Meier: The problem is that no one is dealing with social issues, it's not a question of Modernism or Post-Modernism. There is no public housing built in America and I doubt that there is very much being built in England today. There is no public welfare programme in the United States and those in Europe have declined enormously. There is no public sense of responsibility. This has to do with the climate of our times, which is very unfortunate, and I'm not sure that architecture has the means for changing that attitude.

I'd like to talk about social conscience and all of us being part of the New. The individualism that we have been discussing forms part of what we see in our cities as a common language. Why is it that the individualism that we all know seems to have done less well in all the work of the New Moderns when it comes to large scale housing. This is an area where they all seem to have fallen on their faces even though we admire their work very much as individual performers. I really do think that we are concentrating too much on esotericism.

Daniel Libeskind: First of all, I wouldn't dismiss esotericism so rapidly. If you think of movements such as Christianity or Buddism, they all started as esoteric movements, so that would not invalidate the premises on which esotericism is built. Secondly, I've never had the opportunity to do housing, I'd love to do it, if someone gave me that commission in London.

There is something to a label. Why did the word Deconstruction catch on the way Existential caught on. It's cheap and unimportant in its use, but there is something in the fashion of using that word which in itself testifies to a much deeper desire and a deeper issue. So on both levels, in terms of the fashion and the esotericism, it does not diminish the problem.

Richard Meier: I fear we are all caught in categorisations and, unfortunately, having coined the term and filled it up with a lot of names in travels around the world, it becomes a thing I don't believe is a thing. I don't believe that New Modernism, or whatever you want to call it, is a Movement.

Conrad Jameson: Daniel Libeskind's description of his work in

Berlin is about the most anti-modern tract that I have heard. It is certainly not the philosophy some are getting out of his work. And yet Post-Modernism is a term which Charles Jencks has used to describe both his and Peter Eisenman's work. Isn't the philosophy very similar?

Charles Jencks: I agree that Libeskind and Eisenman are interested in symbolism and in that sense there is the overlap, but the difference between Post Modernists and Neo Modernists is in the decoding: for whom and by whom. For me, the New Modernists are too abstract, too elitist and too complicated. They do not go for the variety of codes that are of the street. They are too restricted, but that does not mean that their intention is not to symbolise. I really think that the work of Fumihiko Maki is important; everything is so beautifully detailed and incredibly well done that suddenly I am a Born Again Modernist. If Modernists don't want to produce alienating buildings they should study the way that Maki does it.

Stuart Lipton: *Can't we accept different architecture, different styles and different materials. Can't we just get on with it, enjoy it, detail it with pleasure?*

Daniel Libeskind: Why don't we just get on with it, detail it, build it and just have a good time? I would like to quote a great Modernist who you are probably familiar with, Charles Baudelaire, where in his preface to the *Flowers of Evil* he wrote the following, 'to get the meaning of these poems (in other words the meaning of life) one is to read Jean-Jacques Rousseau, *Social Contract* and the second way is to take opium, both lead you to some realisation about what I am talking about in the *Flowers of Evil* '. I think if you opt out and go on and say let's just have good time, let's just detail it, then you're just taking a lot of opium. I must say, and so did Charles Baudelaire, it's preferable to read the *Social Contract*.

I'd like to ask Daniel Libeskind if he has an answer to all building types?

Daniel Libeskind: No. Anything as problematic as architecture cannot really deal instrumentally with problem solving, but I think every architect and every student of architecture, who takes this as a challenge, not as an end point, but as a beginning is a very good contributor to the current possibilities. I agree with the comment about the lack of social responsibility. I think it cannot be attributed to architects, but it can be discussed by them. This is the role of architects vis-á-vis the situation. It might very well be that there is something much deeper going on in architecture than simply that scenario of its commissioning or of its immediate task. There is something much deeper going on in architecture other than simply that scenario of its commissioning and of its immediate task, there is a rethinking of the entire field and, in that sense, one might consider in the future that the word architecture may not be used in the same way.

Charles Jencks: Although there is not a complete connection between Neo Modernism and Jewishness, three of its main practitioners happen to be Jewish. In this connection there is a search for historical consciousness.

When you were talking about the idea of Jewish architecture and the architecture of resistance, building up in some form, do you think that could from the basis of a new idea for the avant-garde?

Daniel Libeskind: Anything that seems inevitable is usually not inevitable. Anything which is made by human beings can be redirected, altered, dismantled and laid to rest by human beings, so I don't think one should be too impressed by avant-gardes. One of the disenchanting things is that one is feeling the effects of the human loss of interest and that factor should not be minimised. When people lose interest, they lose interest in certain consistent developments. You call it fashion, but I would just call it loss of interest. If interest is lost everywhere about everything, then I think one has a more interesting debate about what is coming and what has happened already when people have simply lost interest. I think that is what has happened already, people have lost interest in all these things that they believed in.

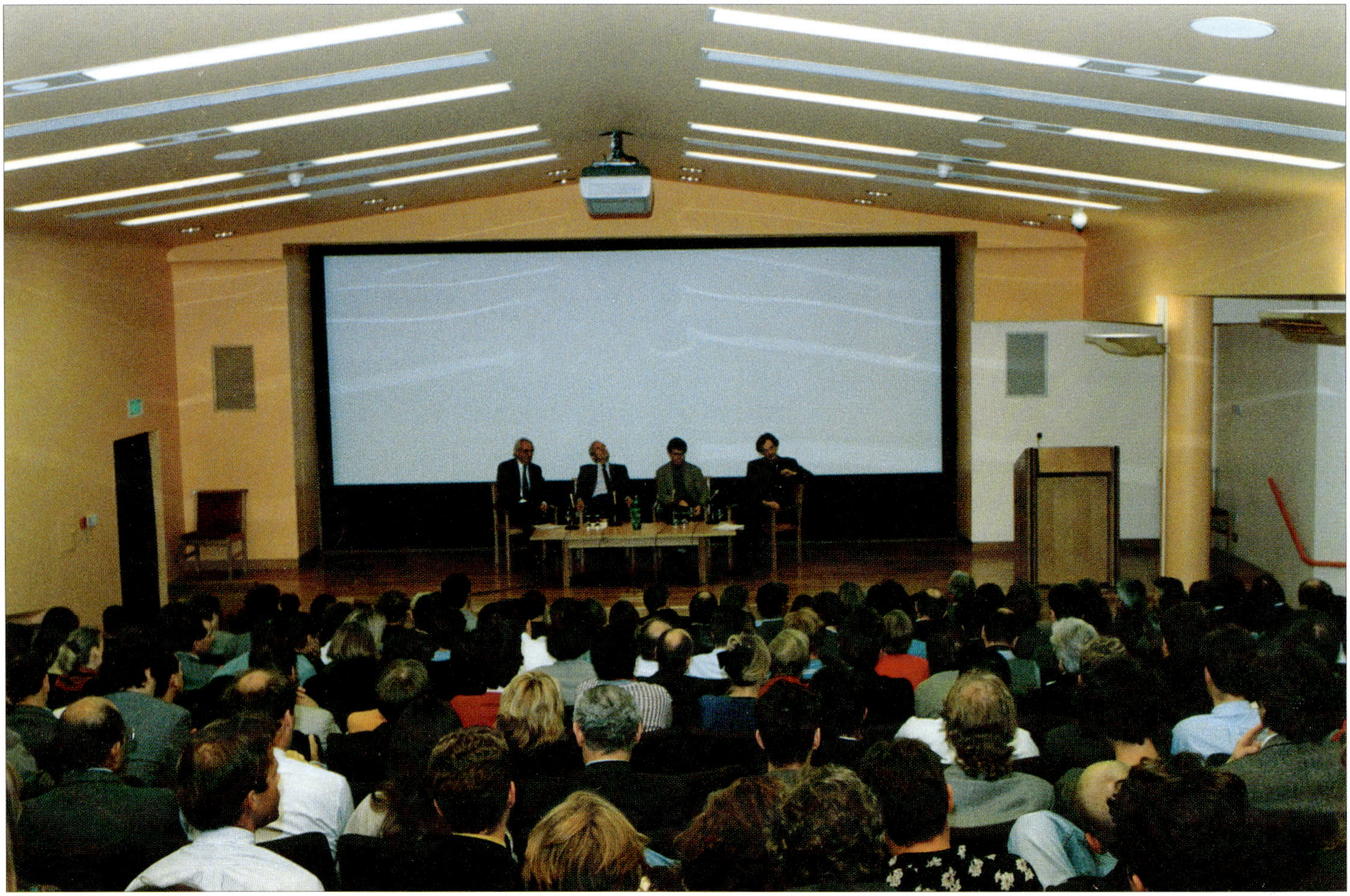

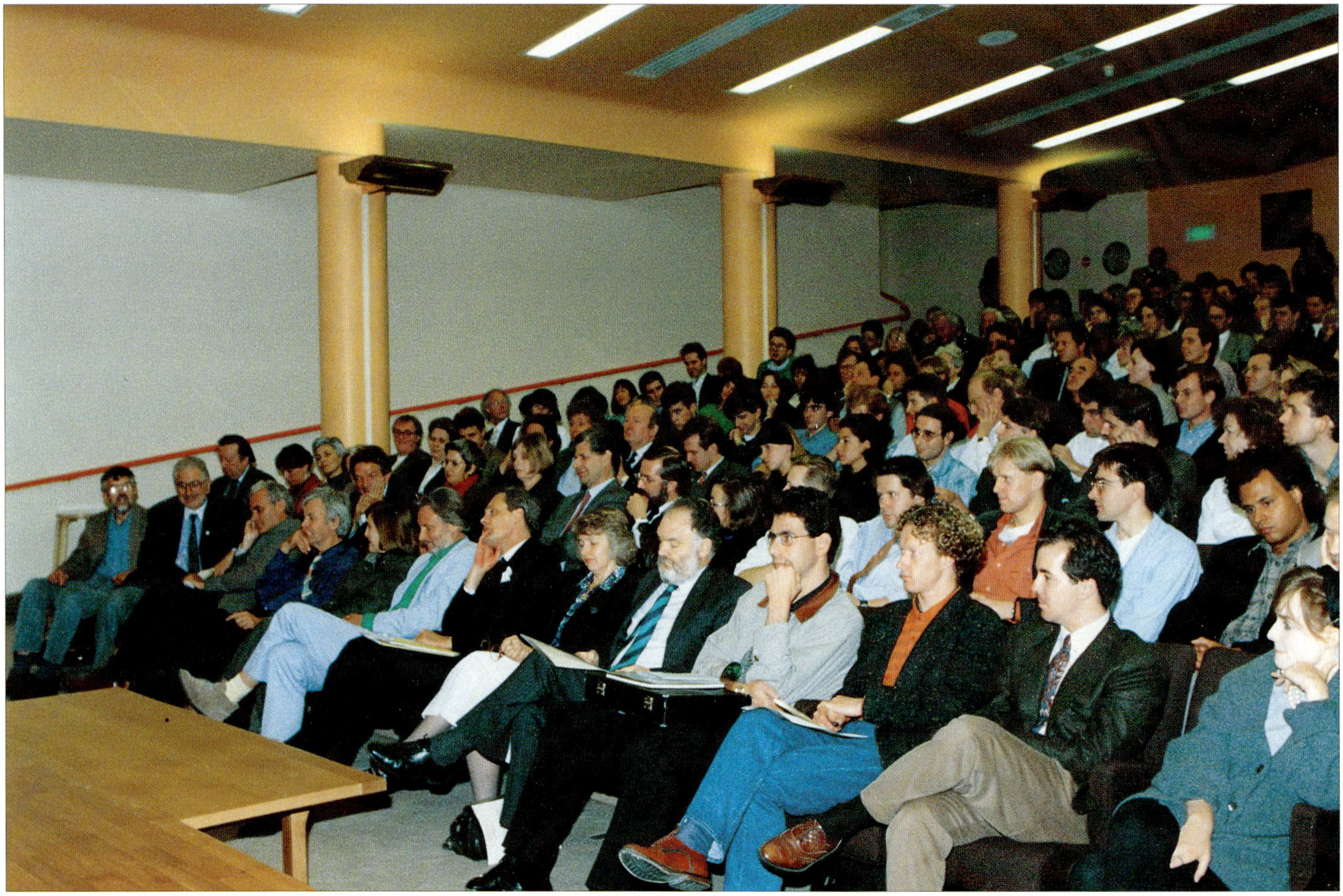

Theme: The New Moderns. *Place*: London. *Date*: September 27, 1990. The second in an annual series examining major issues relevant to the architecture of today, the Forum provides a platform for an international group of architects and critics, allowing the airing of views, whether they be similar, differing or completely contradictory. The previous Forum, held at London's Tate Gallery, had taken as its theme 'A Vision of Britain' – a subject in direct opposition to the one discussed this year.

The Forum, chaired by Paul Finch and Jonathan Glancey, was attended by some thirty participants. It took place without an audience as such but included a number of architectural editors and critics. The afternoon session took its theme from the Symposium at the Tate Gallery on the same evening at which Richard Meier, Daniel Libeskind and Charles Jencks spoke and where questions were raised from the audience.

The following report is an edited account of the afternoon discussion together with written statements by participants, and further enhanced by additional statements written by those who were unable to attend, including Marshall Berman, Conrad Jameson and Kisho Kurokawa.

The two events were extremely thought-provoking and created an interest both with the labelling of 'Modern' and the use of the 'New'. Among the questions raised were: how does the architectural field employ the principles of Modernism in our contemporary world? Does New Modernism exist as a valid architectural label, and can it indeed be thought of as the leading movement of the day? Does the need for a new Modernism merely develop out of a string of styles that have been tried, tested and failed, making Modernism the most recent style to re-New – going back to the future. Perhaps the New Moderns are seen as returning to the image so that the thought process behind the architecture is no different from a new vision, a new classicism or whatever.

It is worth bearing in mind the words of Marshall Berman who states that 'many people are sick of the play. One of the things they are saying is that they want a New Modernism. But I suspect what they're after isn't so much a particular look, sound or style: it's a culture that's serious, that wants to discover and express what's real.' Of course, he also stresses that the way to answer this question is not clear, 'But there are lots of people out there who want an architecture . . . that at least will search for ways to ask. You could call it an architecture that cares.' And because there do exist architects who care and feel it necessary to ask, a Forum such as this can take place.

The New Modernism is another fashionable club created by mass desire and wishful thinking, a club which cruelly accepts only those architects and artists who are not applying. Although many are called by the yearning for a New Movement, only the Decons and the Happy Few are chosen.

A good deal of hype has naturally been written about since the club was first mooted in New York in the early 1980s by Douglas Davis, Ada Louise Huxtable and others. Some arduous youth hoped there would be a revived utopianism, a radical avant-garde, a new socialist cause to which they could fix their banner. Nostalgia for the twenties and the certainties of Modernism in its heyday was palpable. Some old architects hoped their surviving Late-Modern style would miraculously become young; and some middle-aged architects, such as the President of the RIBA, hoped they could fashion a Neo-Mod stick with which to beat the dreaded 'Bimbo Architecture' of Terry Farrell.

But hatred for Post-Modernism does not necessarily a living movement create. Nor does nostalgia for the Age of Revolution create revolutionaries. Hence the confusion of the moment, the desire in excess of performance, the thousands banging on the closed

THE ANNUAL ARCHITECTURE FORUM

Charles Jencks
What is New Modernism?

club door – or to change the metaphor, the thousands desperately looking for the Aluminium Ark, for an object of purity and belief. All these ingredients are likely to produce a pseudo-event, a bandwagon without a band, a will to believe without a belief– and endless journalistic hype. Yet as we know, in the Post-Modern age, media events become self-fulfilling prophecies and if movements are desperately desired to exist, they soon will be fabricated. So be it.

Let the 'New Modernism' begin, if it must, if the young demand a change of heart and the journalists demand a change of theme. Modernism, as Oscar Wilde and Adolf Loos never tired of reminding us, is the pure expression of fashion, of change for its own sake, of the Dionysian ecstasy, of the Futurist orgy of constant renewal – 'Burn what you love, love what you burn' as Nietzsche and Le Corbusier exhorted. Not any particular fashion, but pure fashion, the mechanism of *à la mode*. Who can accept this nihilist programme, who is strong enough to admit this truth? As the Futurist Marinetti said – the archetypal Modern slogan – 'We insist that a masterpiece be burned with the corpse of its author . . . against the conception of the immortal and imperishable we set up the art of becoming, the perishable, the transitory and expendable. There is nothing more expendable and Modern than fashion: each year, like a good Futurist, it clears out the past year's endeavours – what it calls poignantly 'dead stock'.

What could be more nouveau, more up-to-date, raw, topical and novel than the double exocet called, redundantly, the '*New* Modernism', the New New, the Modern Modern? We are so hard of hearing in the TV Age that every statement and programme such as *Mary Hartman, Mary Hartman* has to be repeated, has to be doubled lest it not fire the deadened neurons – in perpetual shock from the latest Shock of the New.

The New New Modern Modern, I might repeat, has nothing to do with white walls, minimalist interiors or the use of perforated metal – all that is journalistic hype necessary to sell papers, the cynical exploitation of a few designers who are modestly trying simply to put one spare material next to another and save their client money. That's all Late-Modernism – worthy, ascetic, well-intentioned but a survival, not something new-new.

No, for the New Mod to exist, if one really wants a new movement, then it must fulfil at least four criteria:

1 It has to answer the critique of Post-Modernism and deal with the previous problems of abstraction, lack of scale and ornament, its anti-urbanism, etc.;

2 In the manner of all 'Neo' movements since 'Neo-Classicism', it has to be a conscious *revival* (not survival) of certain ideas and motifs for a new purpose;

3 It has to have a new philosophy, and

4 a relatively new aesthetic.

From this it is clear that the work of David Chipperfield, Stanton & Williams and Eric Parry – not to mention Richard Rogers, Norman Foster, Nick Grimshaw and Richard Meier – is 'Late' rather than 'Neo', the survival and continuation in a pragmatic way of ideas broached in the 1920s, a vocabulary exaggerated and then subtracted of its utopian message, its socialist philosophy and its progressivist world view. These architects are pragmatists, not revolutionaries: a main motive, in the words of H. H. Richardson, is 'to get the job' – that is, 'to get the capitalists to commission work'. When Modernism went blatantly capitalist – with the Lever House in 1953, or Hong Kong Bank 1986 – then it went blatantly 'Late' however much Bunshaft and Sir Norman might deny the fact. (Let me add, to avoid misunderstanding, that I value Late and Neo-Modernism equally. There is nothing shameful in being tardy, as any Late-Minoan or Late-Baroque architect will tell you – the only real shame comes from pretending one is still like the Modernists of the

"Let the 'New Modernism' begin . . ."

35

twenties, or upholding their social and political ideals. Of course the *materialist* ideals are being continued at a very high level, but the Enlightenment view of social progress has been dropped.)

So who are the real Neo-Mods? According to Criterion One it might be the Japanese Kazuo Shinohara, who has invented a new urbanism based on his reading of Chaos Theory, and Fumihiko Maki, who has created a new ornament and small-scaled Machine Aesthetic based on three things: the small tool revolution, the computer and mass supervision by many assistants. According to Criterion Two it might be the Neo-Constructivists Rem Koolhaas, Zaha Hadid, Frank Gehry and Bernard Tschumi since they have very self-consciously revived 1920s forms and ideas for a hedonistic purpose.

According to Criterion Three, it would obviously be Peter Eisenman who has imported one new idea after another into architecture until he finally turned the old humanist Modernism on its head with Deconstruction and other anti-humanist philosophies garnered from Foucault. Positive nihilism really is new to Modern architecture and if you aren't a nihilist of one kind or another – if you don't have the courage to admit this metaphysic – then there's no room in the tiny clubhouse for you. John Hejduk and Danny Libeskind, keepers of the non-faith, are forever designing monuments to emptiness – especially in that quintessential Neo-Mod city, Berlin. Dealing with the Holocaust, the destruction, uprooting and death that has been *caused by modernisation* are the main themes of the New New. It's iconography.

Hence also the aesthetics of destruction, of what Morphosis calls 'Dead-Tech', that is, heavy metal members smashed up, rusted and then polished to *show* technology always deteriorates. So much for progress, so much for the white dream of the twenties – if you want to practise the NEW-NEW-MOD-MOD-MODE then, like Coop Himmelblau, get out your dynamite, grab some acid, smash across your structures – deconstruct – and then polish the result with a uniform colour. Such is the new aesthetic. It can also be, of course, a new poetic with possibly other hedonistic meanings as one of the few British Neo-Modernists, Peter Wilson, shows in his highly tense juxtapositions of form.

But the decentered, anti-humanist work of the Deconstructionists is the heart of this movement that denies a heart. Its nihilism and frenzied cacophony are really *new* to Modernism. It has challenged the old liberal paradigm, whether it is the humanism of Le Corbusier's Modular Man or the efficiency of Foster's 'doing more with less'. Critics and historians have a duty to distinguish what is vital and real in a movement from what is attached to it by fellow-travellers and journalists: of course, however, the movement will soon be devoured by its followers, by those who have a vested interest in associating themselves with something they take to be pure, and fashionable. And when fashion devours its young we will be onto the next cycle of New.

There is a central paradox to this emergent tradition, and it lies at the heart of all Modernisms since the avant-garde was formed in the 1820s. I will try to explain part of it tonight, but let me raise the conundrum now. The question is: How is it that the New Moderns, or the avant-garde, always presents itself as a 'culture of resistance' – as the outsider – when it has become the dominant culture? How can the Modernists be both radicals and rulers of the Establishment – the RIBA, the Museum of Modern Art – for forty years? How can the Neo-Mods legitimise their deconstruction if, like Bernard Tschumi, they get the *Légion d'Honneur* from Mitterrand, become head of New York City's most prestigious architectural school and become the gadfly of the international circuit? I last met Bernard in Tokyo at the New Otani hotel, where he, Ronald Reagan and I were staying. Reagan was getting $2 million for his efforts, Bernard and I a bit less, but we are all parts of a conflictive Establishment. Post-Modernists admit and take responsibility for this; Neo-Mods hide their complicity behind radical-chic. Why? Is there something, as I believe there is, beyond a quite obvious self-serving hypocrisy? To put the contradiction most dramatically, why, if the Modernists come from the bourgeoisie – if 98 percent are born and remain middle class – must they do everything to deny this existential condition, to attack it in style and content? I hope to answer this conundrum tonight.

* * *

The New Modern architecture exists as both a fashion and movement – as the articles collected here illustrate – and we might distinguish these two motives sharply. Both are important. Without the 'life of forms in art', as Henri Focillion called them, we would never have our appetite renewed, we would be satiated once we ate the first course of architecture. No one likes to admit this truth of fashion, except perhaps its creators, for they know how dependent they, and we, are on the new, on the 'life of forms'. Dead forms, puzzles we have long-ago tired of solving, forms which we know all too well, recede into the unconscious to moulder until they are sufficiently forgotten to be revived. So a motive in the New Modernism is simply this excitement about what is refreshed, or dredged up from the Old Modernism in a new way.

Of equal importance, and likely to be obscured by fashion and all the ideological wrangle over yet *another* Modernism, is the profound reassessment underway within the tradition of the avant-garde. For the first time Modernists are coming to terms with what Marshall Berman calls 'the tragedy of development', the destructive/constructive cycles which underline modernity and the bourgeois class in general. We can see this reassessment in the writings of David Harvey, or more generally, in the reconsiderations of socialism which are coming from Central and Eastern Europe.

Let us make no mistake about the importance of this rethinking. It is global, it comprehends the whole of what is called portentously 'the Modern project' – from the Enlightenment to philosophical positivism, from Marxism to Capitalism, from industrialism to post-industrialism. It will take many years, but the reassessment is starting and now most important from *within* the tradition. This is one positive result of the Post-Modern critique. Hence, in architecture, the complex thematic buildings of Peter Eisenman and Daniel Libeskind, buildings which acknowledge history, symbolism, and the 'destructive/constructive' schizophrenia of the Modern Project. These buildings and a few writings reveal the more serious side to a movement which is also – and necessarily – a fashion.

The architectural label is a necessary evil. It is difficult to begin talking about buildings unless you have a starting point. If you say that the new office block is Post-Modern, it eventually calls to mind a steel framed behemoth clad in fancy panelling. This might be a crude use of a label but it has an immediate image and an immediate value. Labels are unreliable tools when it comes to architectural criticism – think of how we use the term Neo-Classicism and then fascism, and then put the two together. Because your reasonable viewing of history might be limited, you will end up saying Neo-Classical architecture is fascist, because fascists built, of course, Neo-Classical architecture. And the corollary is true if fascist architecture is Neo-Classical. But once you begin to look beyond the immediate labels, you see slogans and slogans conveniently fit the loose association of ideas. Just think for a second of the architecture of Nazi Germany. Hitler

CHARLES JENCKS
Fashion and Reassessment

". . . New Modernism is simply this excitement about what is refreshed . . . "

JONATHAN GLANCEY

"The architectural label is a necessary evil."

liked Neo-Classical buildings and he used to draw them; he certainly commissioned them. Would you say that he was a Neo-Classicist? Hitler thought that civic buildings should be classical and that *hausen*, outside cities should be *vogueisch*, or what we might call neo-vernacular or romantic pragmatist. So perhaps Hitler was a romantic pragmatist or a Neo-Classicist. Are young architects inspired by Modernism or a nostalgia for Modernism? Whether it is principles or it is appearances. Are they Neo-Moderns because they build in a modern style? Is Norman Foster a Modern? Is he a Late-Modern? Is he a Neo-Modern? Is he a Hi-Technician? Or is he just an architect's accountant responsible for a particular programme, in his own particular way with his own architects?

My feeling is that labels have their uses but labels also actively encourage kitsch, both in ideas and in building. Most architecture, certainly in Britain over the past ten years, has been led not by the people in this room, but by commercial property developers. British building types of the 1980s have been: the speculative office block, the shopping mall and the out of town super-store. Because the programme of these buildings is simplistic, the architecture is that of costumier or couturier, and like anyone involved in the fashion business, the label on the back of the jacket is what counts. So the architects that have been most recently have been fancy dress Post-Modernists, fancy dress Neo-Classicists, fancy dress new vernacularists – encouraging a new label in Modern – and we will see quite quickly a rush of buildings in whatever style that is, or whatever style happens to fit its definition.

The allusive shape of our city centres are architectural wallpaper for the most part, designed in drag, often with backing from civic clients, with specific needs, their financiers don't want these sort of buildings anyway. They want the latest convention and that can be any style you like. These architects flounder in a sea of styles. I don't know how many Daniel Libeskind style museums will be built in the next few years but I am sure they will start to appear. I don't know whether they are New Modern or not. I think office blocks and shopping malls built in that style are already on the way because people have seen them published in magazines. Create labels for architects with a clear vision of where they are heading, but keep them under your hat.

". . . architects flounder in a sea of styles."

The strength of the Modern Movement in architecture is at least partly the result of its embrace of new materials and technologies, and its willingness to rise to the challenge of designing new building types. This has been the cause of problems – particularly where architecture has been ahead of the technology, leading to failures in what would otherwise have been not merely iconic buildings, but technically successful iconic buildings. Hence the familiar headlines about award-winning buildings whose roofs leak. The growth of a new bold and experimental attitude in contemporary architecture is partly due to technology catching up with, and indeed overtaking, what it is that architects may be imagining; or alternatively, that it is possible to test innovative ideas to destruction before putting them into permanent built form. It is no accident that many of the buildings that have made most impact on the public in recent years have owed much of their development to the work of structural and services engineers, from the Hong Kong Bank to the Hôtel du Département at Marseille.

PAUL FINCH

This is not merely to do with hi-tech architecture, or as it looks like becoming, the deployment of extremely complex technical ideas to produce low-technology, low-energy architecture. It is surely conceivable that in the not-too-distant future, developments in glass technology, already with us in experimental form, will transform the ability of the architect to play with light, and hence with volumes and massing in entirely new

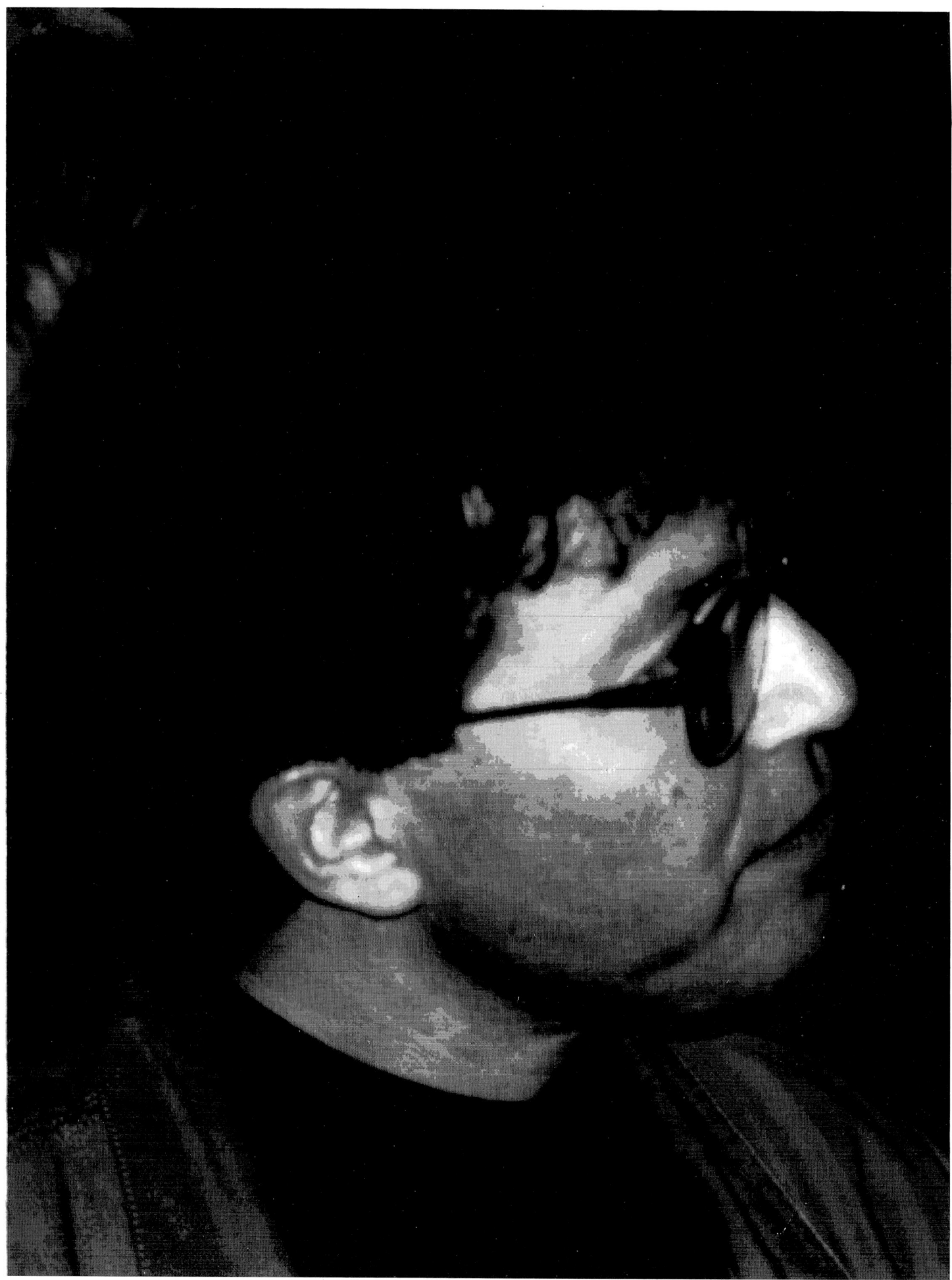

ways. This is the result of diachronic glass on the one hand, and structural glass on the other. I think we can imagine which architectural tendency will wish to maximise the potential of such materials, not least because it will be possible to produce a new architecture on at least one of those wet Monday mornings . . .

The relationship between building technology and architecture has its own history, which one could argue is oblivious to the development of other design styles; one could trace the ideas of an architect like Foster from his earliest buildings without making any reference to Post-Modernism. That presumably would exclude him from the category of the Neo-Modernists, though this may look curious if and when his Tokyo Tower gets built.. Perhaps it will be Neo-Late Modern by then. In the meantime, it is possible to challenge the notion that the pruning effects of criticism are what have allowed Modernism to reflourish. There is a strong whiff of 'post hoc ergo propter hoc', which is no more acceptable in architectural history than it is in any other branch.

Madrid today: Peking yesterday: Leningrad tomorrow . . .

No sooner has one begun a work – touched pen to paper – then the effort lapses, inseminates itself with another one, cancels and overcomes its origins, begets endings that are interminably longer than its own previous history. Incorporating the undecidable in a uniquely proliferating system of displacements, architecture's groundlessness finally becomes ours, becomes a state one no longer hopes to be rid of: abysmal, still more weighty: an obelisk that cannot stifle the spreading desert. A mechanism that reaches what 'no eye ere grieved for', distressing in its effects, causing the indifference of unrelieved vigilance, virtuous and subversive at once.

Until today, Architecture was on the wrong track. 'Rising up to heaven or grovelling on the ground, it has misunderstood the principles of its existence and has been, not without reason, constantly derided by upright folk. It has not been modest . . . the finest quality that ought to exist within an imperfect being'. Since its very appearance Architecture sought to construct mechanically the brain of stupefied dwelling. But it was not sufficient to mimic language (history and meaning) in order to create a place which is *not* wherever the calculating, mocking smile of the constructor *is*.

Architectural thought no longer exists – no longer exists as a self-deferential discourse, no more than does any other autobiography. Permanently infecting the maternal sources which render identity, technique itself contaminates the sense of dwelling across language, introduces mechanisms of transference between architecture and subject, reprieves fatherhood in the sense of conscious begetting . . . Rending architectural mother-tongue by violating its limit, haunting the abrasive traceable which had its beginning in a dawning of guilt, architecture becomes past in the sense that today it has entered its code. A code EX, a coded that cannot be decoded; an X, a CODEX which invalidates its origin/ality raises the un/original, founded as it is upon incertitude, upon the void, upon the language of the dead which yet refuses to be a monument to a dead language. There will be no more specialists in provoking grandeur through power, no fictitious images which would have been better to soothe their author's brain, no beams raised high above mortal existence. Eyes will revert to themselves on completion of the investigation and will perceive the grace of someone struggling to steady himself, herself.

The skeleton hanging: the carcass. The uncertainty of muscular movements in wounds or in the soft parts of the lower cerebral regions. Ultraviolent cities. Here X: *con architettura* . . . Lobsters in the Russian Stables. *Ex-con*: architecture. Camels under the ecumenical banner of the perpetually trapped, perpetually reset by the trapped rat, analogical *polis*.

". . . architecture has its own history . . ."

Daniel Libeskind
Countersign

"Architectural thought no longer exists . . ."

By disarticulating boundaries architecture's beauty comes to be identified with its congenital malformation. The result of aesthetic principles which have varied and will vary again, but not in accordance with the progress of mankind. Is the process annulling the traces of intellectual disturbances which hark back to the spherical and convex surface area which resembles an orange only in shape?

Nothing remains except deference: the deference of the immortals to the immortelles. Documents only map the neurotic ground which under the insignia of reason/foundation/nation usurps the ever unreadable yet ever re-consecrated text. Every community is questionable, and questionable precisely in its deadening, politically pre-arranged disappointments. The architect's refusal to indulge in the paradise of recirculated enchantment – in myth – paranoia – leads to a not-etymological, a-historical, foundation-less architecture; one moreover produced in a time of renewed anti-international and national crises.

Max Hutchinson

" There is certainly not a Modernist Mafia."

Q: As a representative of the establishment, Max Hutchinson, is there a Modernist establishment still? Is there a new Modernist establishment emerging?
I don't think there is a Modernist establishment. There is certainly not a Modernist Mafia. For example, architect's education is not being carefully administered and orchestrated for some sort of Late Modernist anti Post Modernist cause. It is an absolute fabrication. I do sense that in a predominantly middle class generation, a genuinely younger generation, certainly younger than anyone else in this room, there is a renewed fascination with some of the things that Charles Jencks has talked about – certainly with materials, material technology and the way in which those early Modernist principles can be brought together with a renewed social pragmatism. That has flourished in young people in education and in immediate post-education in a way which we did not notice a few years ago. We were preoccupied with the sort of commercial style conversations which Jonathan Glancey talked about. The application of what I call *The Wall* , most commercial architecture is skin thick, it is only about the wall. If you talk to the Bovis technologists that put together Broadgate and are now putting together Canary Wharf, they talk about the wall, they talk about the structure and separately about the wall. When they come to talk about the wall, they mean the architecture.

While we have been preoccupied with that, discussing and debating it, young people have become genuinely fascinated with the technology which is inspired by their bedroom; it is the same technology they find with their walkman, their private computer and their synthesizer. They are the midi generation, the floppy disc generation. They have no conscience about that. They bring that freshness and that enquiring mind that I feel is fresh and new. They have a freshness and a naivety which we should encourage, and which the best of architectural education and, indeed, the RIBA actually does encourage.

"They are the midi generation, the floppy disc generation."

Geoffrey Broadbent

I'd find it easier to recognise the 'New Moderns' if I knew who the old ones were. Le Corbusier was at least five architects, Wright perhaps seven and very different. Mies was only one for most of his career yet different again. Le Corbusier and Gropius too had their social, even Utopian, visions: 'We know how you should live and we have ways of making you live like that.' Mies also looked for the perfect new material: 'weatherproof, soundproof . . . insulating (and) light.' The laws of physics don't allow it so he used glass instead; thus expressing the 'spirit of the – machine, everything factory-made – age.' This spirit, of course, could also be expressed by applying into architecture two kinds of art

44

unknown before the 20th century: geometric abstraction and machine-forms. Le Corbusier and others constructed them, of traditional building materials, in the white-walled villas of the 1920s. But they didn't work. They streaked, stained and cracked, the roofs leaked and intelligent architects abandoned them.

Those intelligent architects too: Le Corbusier, the Bauhaus lehrer, the Constructivists had attitudes to the programme or the brief, summed up by: 'A house is a machine for living in.' So they analysed architecture as if it were engineering. Amazingly enough it worked in such Modern masterpieces as Le Corbusier's Clarté Apartments in Geneva, his Ministry of Education in Rio, Terragni's Casa del Fascio. Each was designed to house certain functions, at a particular location, with a particular climate, responding, even, to a particular sun-path. And they changed from white plaster to marble, or glittering, irregular white mosaic (Terragni); stone slabs, later board-marked concrete and chunky brickwork (Le Corbusier).

I see none of this self-questioning, this response and responsibility, in the work of the 'New Moderns'; no engineer-like analysis of programmes, nor even Utopian visions; indeed little to connect them to their heroes but nostalgic repetitions of those white-walled geometric abstractions, those machine-forms, which the Masters had abandoned by the end of the 1920s. And some New Moderns seem to be searching still for a pure, anti-Physics, smooth, white, jointless, magic material that will stay perfect and unsullied till the end of time. So it is, they wander back to the future!

Richard Meier

The Modern Movement questioned the prevailing attitude of slavishly recreating the past. It yanked architecture out of the padded yoke of popular opinion, out of the comfortable despair of the banal. It changed the way we look and think about architecture so that ideas about place, use, materials and technology are related to ideas about *form, proportion, light,* and *scale.* In striving to broaden the morphogenetic field, technology became paramount. But, it is as if in their love affair with the machine, with the cool light of the purely rational, they lost touch with the sensual, the ground of our aesthetic being. The heroic mind overwhelmed *its own* spiritual vision, for when the idea of the machine replaces the idea of the mind's eye and the architect's hand, there comes that deep alienation of man from his environment. Whereas the Modern masters seemed to our eyes to be too rigidly identified with the idea and potential of mass production, of industrial man, this is now a fact of life, simply one of a number of resources at the architect's disposal. We now assume the tectonic and spatial authority of the Modern Movement, each new miracle of building holds only limited fascination. For me, technology is no longer the subject of architecture, but simply the means. Architecture is the subject of my architecture.

"Architecture is the subject of my architecture."

Abstraction in architecture continues to be one of the most powerful legacies of the Heroic Period. It continues to provoke us to invent and to elaborate on ways to geometrically organise and interpret human activities. Distinct and completely evolved plastic systems such as De Stijl, Purism and Constructivism each embodied the thought that architecture was important and dealt with aspects of the machine and the poetry of space. Today, the most compelling extension of that impulse towards abstraction is Deconstructivism. I feel akin to the embrace of the purely sculptural. I applaud the evocative focus on intellectual commitment. However, the nature of their inquiry and the quality of their objects *inevitably* collide with my concerns for the particularities of scale and place. There is no place for the physical in the Decons' intriguing network of forces. The web of their universe exists in a mind clearly alienated from the hierarchy and order essential to habitation. Nonetheless, I defend the validity and vitality of their speculation on the unreal. What I seek to do is to pursue the plastic limits of Modern Architecture to include a notion of beauty moulded by light. My wish is to create a kind of spatial lyricism within the canon of pure form.

In the design of my buildings, I am expanding and elaborating on what I consider to be the formal basis of the Modern Movement. What the 20th century did was create the ability to crack open an otherwise classically balanced plan. The spirit of the 20th century is allowed to go in and out through that crack, so that the experience of being in the building is not static, but everchanging.

This 20th century fissure made possible by the free plan, the free facade, the separation of structure and skin, the whole formal basis of the Modern Movement, fostered a new kind of volumetric exploration, one that still seems to hold many possibilities.

The great promise and richness of some of the formal tenets of Modernism have almost unlimited areas for investigation.

My work does not lie within the Neo-Classical tradition, I reject the representational and embrace the abstract. Mine is a preoccupation with space, not scaleless space, but space whose order and definition are related to light, to human scale and to the culture of architecture. Architecture is vital and enduring because it contains us; it describes space, space we move through, exist in and use.

"I manipulate forms in light . . ."

I work with volume and surface; I manipulate forms in light, changes of scale and view, movement and stasis.

My sources include many from the history of architecture, but my quotes and allusions are never literal; my meanings are always internalised, my metaphors purely architectural. I am still taken with the poetics of Modernism, the beauty and utility of technology. My primary ordering principles have to do with a kind of purity that derives in part from the inherent distinction between the man-made and the natural. This distinction serves to reunite the two in a complimentary relationship. I see man's intervention as an aesthetic organisation of the environment. I seek to impose a coherent system of mutually dependent values, a harmonious relationship of parts. By this, I mean a resolution of all the interlocking issues of form, function and fitness.

Above all, there has to be a reciprocal involvement between the concept for a building and its physical manifestation. My rigour is a search for clarity.

This search, for me, begins with the plan. The plan which seems to have been neglected of late, is in fact the key. This two-dimensional image contains within it the instructions for the three-dimensional object that is the building. Together with the section, it generates the building. While the elevation tends to pictorialise, the plan and section speak to the architect about spatial ideas. But the plan is the most convincing and fundamental expression of the architectural idea.

". . . buildings should speak."

I believe that buildings should speak. In my work, the use of a specific and internally consistent vocabulary of elements and themes over the years has allowed me a coherent, evolutionary means of expression. The process by which I manipulate and assemble this vocabulary within the urban and historical context has become more complex and comprehensive, an intellectual progression which has coincided with the growing scope and complexity of our recent commissions.

Piers Gough

If Farrell and Stirling disliked being called Post-Modern then how much more the purveyors of White Stuff are going to hate being New Moderns. Any suggestion that

Modernism is a style, particularly one of appearance, has always been anathema. It has always held itself to be based on the twin necessities of belief and brief with architectonic considerations being the abstractions of light and space, solid and void. But the defences of Modernism against being a style rather than coming out of the rigorous pursuit of programme might be said to have been buried some years ago with Foster's 100 alternative models of the BBC.

However, cycles are made to come round and with the sheer quantity of embarrassing and lousy Post-Modernism challenging that of remaining grotty sub-Modernism. Architects' aesthetic persuasions are coming back out of the stained woodwork. Obviously there has been a strong element of continuing commitment to Modernism here, heroically by the Hi-techs and tastefully by the thirty-somethings. Post-machine style can deliver thrills, but it is hard to look forward to more buildings whose claim to the New Age is simply to be stripped and white, bearing the same relationship to the Bauhaus as Quinlan Terry to Georgian Architecture.

However, New Modernism sounds a good deal fresher than the grisly Critical Regionalism, a term best used to describe critics not architecture. Perhaps it is only right that with the construction economy on a life-support system, buildings should all look like sanatoria. But as we Interflora the wreaths for Po-Mo let us be thankful that, for a time there, it revelled in admitting that other buildings do already exist, that the art of architecture need not only consist of the rules of reductivism and making things line up, and, that the found form of the city just might have something to teach us if only that the back of the pavement line is for building against. Things *have* changed, even Domus now claims to be contexturalist.

Listening to this discussion does give me an awareness of wanting to don corduroy trousers and a jeans jacket and start talking about the people. It's the literal thing which I adore. Of all the buildings that subvert the human being to a big idea, I would have thought that the Grande Arche is the prime one. If that is a new kind of socialism, I would certainly put it below capitalism. I don't think that there is any doubt that I would prefer to work in the Hong Kong Shang Hai Bank. This is the ultimate irony as it is by a man who professes to design buildings for people and is alleged to start every interview with: 'This particular project is about people'. This I have always found laughable really, because of course, one's image is exactly the opposite to what is probably the truth. The claim to be a humanist aesthete may come from a person who doesn't appear to be so or to operate in that way.

So it worries me beyond belief when people start talking about the solid and void. I just have that feeling, as Richard Meier says, that architecture is all about architecture. The incestuousness of the concern is exquisitely put.

Leon Krier, from what I understand, suggests that architecture lost its way when it became interested in filling stations, and started to imitate them, and claimed they were architecture. He would prefer architecture to be like architecture. Meier would like architecture to be like architecture. I think we all really want architecture to be about architecture. We are all incredibly mannerist, and the only regret I have is that we are mannerist but not baroque. If we are going to be mannerist we are going to need a little less of the self-denial which we all adore and to admit that all we are interested in is architecture. It is a game. Let's play it, with some pleasure!

Q: Leon Krier, is this just a game?
We are obviously playing here with words and I think there is a problem with the new

"New Modernism sounds a good deal fresher than the grisly Critical Regionalsim . . ."

Leon Krier

title. According to the content it should be called the New Modernists or the Modern Modernists. The confusion of modern and Modernist is not so much a mistake but a misappropriation for modern and Modernist have very different meanings. The term modern is a chronological term whereas Modernist has a clear ideological message which applies to the subject matter of this book.

What is evident is that New Modernism is definitely more aesthetically minded and more decorative than Post-War Modernism; it is full of nostalgia of early Modernist buildings and paintings, that is alright perhaps, but we are not here to talk about influences and references. We are here to talk about fundamental values, values which inform buildings, cities, education, and life in general. What I see in these buildings is that they are extremely fragile and flimsy structures; they are truly consumer items which will take one generation to wear out and be thrown away without regret; in rare cases, restored beyond their real life capacity. Maybe there are some great ideas at the basis of Modernism; maybe the open plan, the strip window, the separation of façade and support structure, can produce this or that great building, but they remain exceptional, because it is in the nature of this technique to produce disposable items.

Should we defend Modernism on a pragmatic level and accept a consumer ideology as fundamental condition for Modernism, we must also be aware that such an ideology is extremely destructive of nature, that it is fundamentally anti-ecological and it cannot be a basis for making architecture over a long period of time.

But the greatest fallacy of Modernism is not its principles, materials and technology, but the assumption that these ideas represent the new paradigm, revolutionising, invalidating and replacing all previous architectural traditions, knowledge and techniques. Such attempts at totality not only contradict our ideas of tolerance but of experience, intelligence and education. So far Modernism holds a virtual monopoly over architectural education, and the profession itself is obsessed with maintaining this monopoly. In fifty years not a single traditional architect has been awarded an RIBA gold medal, and that must surely be a sign that something stinks in the small world of the architects. The values of the American Revolution, which are not so much to do with democracy but with tolerance, they are about to shake architecture as well. But tolerance does not mean that we all have to jump into the melting pot. On the contrary, it allows us, while disagreeing , to live side by side without shooting at each other, not to discredit each other professionally because we believe that flat roofs are better and holier than pitched roofs. We as professionals make ourselves simply ridiculous standing in public, bashing our heads, spreading calumny and narrow-mindedness. Modernists seem to be incapable of accepting that Prince Charles should like some buildings of Quinlan Terry and some of Foster. They will only accept his admiration for Foster's King's Cross terminal as genuine if he condemned at the same time what I am doing. Curiously, I have the feeling that Modernism was interesting and produced some interesting results and poetry when it was a minority movement in the early 20s. It is at this moment again more interesting and aesthetic precisely because, under the avalanche of criticism started by Prince Charles, it has simply to try harder to be accepted. Modernists, and above all students, seem to be moved by the idea of newness. But where and how does newness occur, where is it relevant and where is it necessary? Do you have to push the limits of architecture forward on all fronts . We ourselves are created by a genetic system which is extremely old yet is capable of producing unseen newness with every newborn. That is the kind of newness that real traditional architecture is capable of. Of course there is typological innovation which is determined by new uses. But innovation is not a *goal* in

" . . . the greatest fallacy of Modernism is not its principles . . ."

" . . . innovation is not a goal . . ."

Michael Wilford

itself, it is a *means* to find solutions which need not necessarily be new. Over the last two centuries new building types have been developed as a response to new uses such as power stations airports, filling stations, etc. In the XIX century, railway terminals found an adequate building type which served well for over 100 years. Strangely, airports were not so lucky and the reason why they are in constant reconstruction and reshaping is that they have not yet evolved an adequate typological answer to their function. Maybe Foster's Stanstead and Jahn's Chicago 'United' terminals go towards such a real type, which in its vastness will be able to embrace the inner changes without necessarily having to undergo complete reconstruction. In that sense, they are truly classical and traditional buildings because they extend the typological family and they are no more machines than the traditional house or temple. If they really are, they will also reach a certain stability and permanence. This is very far indeed from the quasi religious 'flexibility dogma' revered by Cedric Price. Change in architecture is a necessity for as long as you have not found the adequate solution to a problem. Change for changes' sake is an idiotic attitude. You don't change your wife because it is fashionable but because you don't love her. If after years of search and work you have finally the piano you have been dreaming of, you will not dispose of it for changes' sake. It will be so good in matter of touch, sound, colour and form that it gives you renewed and unequalled pleasure everyday. The same is true for buildings, towns and landscapes. In the search for quality, the idea of Modernism is quite irrelevant, whether we design houses, aeroplanes or cities.

Q: Some people say that Stirling-Wilford themselves may have become Modernist.
Most of these questions ought to be addressed directly to my partner, James Stirling. As a practising architect and also as a teacher, I am very concerned about the impact that some of those messages have on most of the profession and on most of the students in the architectural schools. I suppose I am asking questions about the extent to which what I read and what I hear is actually relevant to practising architecture. I hear and see a good deal of environmental arrogance and more so intellectual masturbation – very introspective writing and graphics which I don't understand. I ask myself what really is inadequate about seeking to make an architecture which has a straight forward function of fulfilling cultural objectives. I suppose a lot of discussion is about trying to find appropriate cultural information. But still I am appalled about what I read and hear about anti-humanism and disorganisation. It seems to me we ought to make our buildings comprehensible to the public at large – 98 percent of the public do use these buildings. For me, whilst that has to be the basic functional satisfaction, the building must do all the things that have been mentioned: they must have light, they must have air, they must be warm and they must evidently support the activity for which they have been built. It seems to me that particularly public buildings have to have a basic clarity of organisation. If people get lost they must soon be able to find their way around the building. There has to be secondary and tertiary layers of interest in the place. It is a kind of layering process. I think architecture is mainly about making spaces and about making coherence of them.

For us the technologies and the materials that are now available, are really a means to an end, rather than an end in themselves. I think a lot of the buildings that are recently being completed, illustrate what seems to me, the using of material structure and systems as a primary expressive element of the architecture rather than, as I say, a supportive element, something that is actually a fundamental coherent.

I think to address your question – Charles Jencks is very fond of actually making tables and diagrams by which you can trace currents, not only by individual architects but also by groups of architects. We have on the wall of our office, not a table by Jencks, but one very similarly which is produced by a Swiss group, which actually sets out the buildings and the calendar. The table indicates the kind of constant overlapping of ideas and expressions. We try to combine abstraction and representation in our buildings, we are not all for one or for the other. It is constant striving to integrate both aspects so that the building is very much an expression of its time or the values of that time.

The question asked is 'whether there really is a new Modern architecture today and, if so, which directions it will pursue.' The question follows the publication in Berlin of *Eine postmoderne Moderne*, also suggesting that deconstruction is perhaps 'part of the modern in Post-Modernism.' By so saying, it is implied that deconstruction is the latest form of Modernism, or 'Late-Modern'.

Aside from those aspects of deconstruction that might be said to belong to Modernism it seems to us that signs of a new architecture have emerged in the work of certain deconstructionist architects, such as Tschumi or Koolhaas, and in other recent works by young architects.

The question that must therefore be asked is whether this is simply a different kind of formal expression, or whether the difference goes deeper than that and whether we are, in fact, faced with an architecture beyond Modernism. More generally speaking, a different conceptual approach is to be noted in Deconstruction, which takes account of a wider and more open system of references when addressing the usual range of functional or technical constraints. For instance: Are not new systems of aesthetic references apparent when Shinohara suggests that: 'Many people use as a working principle the idea that a confused, disorderly city is attractive'? In such a case, in recent buildings by certain Japanese architects, volumes and forms are put together in a seemingly chaotic way, for example Kazuo Shinohara in the T I T Centennial Hall and more recently Makoto Sei Watanabe in Sea Vista or in the Ore-x Angel Complex.

Are not the new systems of relationship between space and its limits apparent when the entire facade of a building is a single suspended film of glass, with wind bracing provided by a structure set two metres in front of it? In such a case, the physical and visual limits of space are totally dissociated, as seen for instance in the facade of the BPOA building in Rennes.

Is not a new system of spatial organisation apparent when movement is the only means of perceiving space, and the time taken by this movement the only means of establishing the function – or functions – allocated to that space? An example can be seen in the reception and service functions of the Cité des Sciences extended over the whole of Parc de la Villette by the implantation of Bernard Tschumi's system of follies.

These three examples – and they are not the only ones – we regard as evidence revealing the emergence of something new and different in architecture. This new kind of architectural phenomenon must be analysed to determine which category it springs from. Is it simply an evolution of Modernism itself, or are we faced with the emergence of a deeper mutation, heading beyond Modernism?

Is it simply an evolution of the means of expressing a Modernism which leaves the basic principles untouched, or are we witnessing the beginning of a rupture with Modernism and, if so, of the building up of premises for new rules; a new logic and new architectural thinking? A certain number of factors which have progressively yet profoundly transformed the way space is perceived and conceived might be considered as portents

Odile Decq

" . . . volumes and forms are put together in a seemingly chaotic way . . ."

leading to the appearance of change:

– New techniques for representing and visualising space, in parallel with the different ways of seeing space offered by film, greatly changed the relationship of forms and the relationship of space and time.

– New means and techniques for computing, in parallel with the evolution of means of using materials, make different structures possible and give a new freedom in relation to technical constraints.

– Evolution of mathematical, physical and biological theories, in parallel with the growth of worldwide communications.

These three factors are far from sufficient to explain the feeling that a change is emerging in the perception of Modernism. Several trends coexist within deconstruction itself, for example, Coop Himmelblau's Attic Conversion in Vienna – with its seemingly deconstructed expressionist structure – should not be analysed in the same way as Rem Koolhaas' Centre for Art and Media technology at Karlsruhe, with its very polished appearance; but within which the functional and spatial organisation is radically different.

Nigel Coates

Q: Do you think that buildings should last forever?

I am always asked whether buildings should last forever. I never expect a building to last by itself. What you see is not going to last forever, its going to be ripped out and painted white. I feel the same sense of dismay. It is not an accident that this isn't also in a19th-century institution. Eventually we are talking about a fight between modern influence and traditional influence. I would say again that I can only subscribe to the notion of the modern if we really do embrace the modern world we live in. At the moment I am fit to decline whether we are dealing with space, volume and respecting the Modernists. I personally don't care about that. What I do care about is the language of the present day. Buildings are built and knocked down for economic reasons anyway. In five years, 25 percent of Tokyo is rebuilt. You can build a building to last as long as you like, but it will be demolished as soon as it becomes economical to do so.

Cedric Price

We virtually have just designed the label for a range of air structures that actually says *used by* and there is a date on it. Now we are not designing food for a supermarket that is the essential part of the architectural design of a short life building.

* * *

– The Villette multi-floored truck park/Science Museum should be in Tschumi-red panels without a door.

– My glasshouse is partly sub-terranean to accommodate plants in excess of Tschumi height limits.

– Against my site the level of the dock water varies to accommodate this limitation – should my glass house float?

– One cannot see into the glasshouse nor when in, see out.

– The nature of wit, humour and style in architecture is a function of the nature of its users, no more than that.

– Concern with defining the limits of the discipline of architecture is a trap which is part of the function of the trapped.

– The common acceptance of paradox and uncertainty threatens architects because of its very commonality.

– The serious folly is safe – safe folly a lie.

– The eagerness of architects to be understood is too shrill a sound for the sagacious and too late a sound for the dreamer.

– 'The idea of place cannot be made precise' *Russell.*

– The acceptance of imprecision by most, in the understanding and appreciation of architecture is deemed threatening by the ignorant.

Marcus Binney

Buildings may have been designed to have been destroyed. Prefabs were designed not to last, but they went on for years and years, and, in some cases, they are still there. It is inevitable that things which may have been seen as temporary come to be valued more; that is why the Barcelona Pavillion has been reconstructed, because it is seen as more important than simply a temporary exhibition. It is arrogant to say that my buildings are designed to go; I do not want them to be preserved. Once you have built them they have been launched on the scene. It is up to the people to judge them, value them, use them and decide.

Robert Adam

Q: What do you think of the language of the present day? Have we written classicism out of style?

What really fascinates me is this absolute fear of style. It is a development of the Modernist idea to destroy style forever. In fact educationally it is very difficult to use the word style. The thing, is it is inevitable. A column needs to understand what you see. I go along with the theory that the world is essentially chaotic and the only way to make any sense of it at all is to categorise things. If you can't imagine what you going to categorise with Modernism, then you will be in total relapse. You jolly well will be! Style is only a categorisation, only a consistent association of certain visual features – the way that you might identify things so that you can even talk about them.

It is philosophically extremely interesting, it is an interesting to talk about. There are far too many interesting things to talk about. The problem is just about everyone, that's people in the profession, probably can't be bothered. And as the result of that the meaning is debased of all the things we are talking about the New Modern is probably random. I can't stand the idea that modern as modern has been hijacked by Modernism as an expression. It removes art still further from common understanding. I see that as the greatest tragedy in Modernism, of the 20th century that is the age of Modernism, and of Neo-Modernism as well as anything else, and of Post-Modernism which I am not particularly fond of. I believe that Modernism is just an aspect of that elitist form of socialism which existed in the 20s and 30s where you told people what they liked. I believe that the New Moderns are really just an exasperation of this appalling situation as they are a development of the same kind of thing, perhaps a mannerist development of it. They are the real culprits for the appalling general standard in design and they are the culprits for the state of the public interest, understanding and involvement in it, the intellectual activities do not have to be elitist and arcane. The parallel I have made many times and will make again is that we are all like Aristotle's helmsmen, responsible for the loss of our ship whilst absent from the helm.

Stephen Games

" One can be Modern yet not Modern . . . A lovely paradox."

Q: Has architectural discussion lost interest in architecture?

Architectural discussion like this is actually fascinating. One can be modern yet not Modern, one could be producing architecture at two a day and yet not be Modern. A lovely paradox. And naturally when you lay that paradox on the table, it is an invitation to carry on playing with it and tossing it around, forever. It can never be resolved. There are a number of ways of approaching architecture. There are any number of approaches of forms of interpretation. You have to plan in advance every time a building is built, what the intellectual system is that you are going to have to plug into that building in order to understand it. So, I am suspicious of one system of thought displacing all others. I would like to see the frontiers of architecture being pushed forward by architects rather than critics. Finally, my concern is that when thinking about architecture becomes a scholastic game, it makes architects look silly. We are wanting in more approaches to architecture. This meeting, however, is not about architecture, it is about ways of understanding and interpreting architecture.

It's no longer a question of saying what is good of the modern, here we were supposed to say what is good of the New Modern. I am incredibly fascinated by the New Modern. I think what is New in Modern is that architects are more important than architecture. Because architects are more important than architecture; every architect is trying to be himself, or the solution that he is inventing. They are beautiful and they produce wonderful drawings, but an artist is not an architect.

Henri Ciriani

". . . an artist is not an architect."

* * *

BECAUSE
Somebody must represent the 'Old Modern',
BECAUSE
I am a confirmed optimist,
I ACCEPT to participate in the forum and trust this 'New Moderns' title to the symposium is not simply another label coined to represent a new set of graphics but a progressive move.
BECAUSE
Due to the fact that the word 'building' means in English both action and the object, it has been difficult to know where architecture lay, or what it was, up to the latest trend: Industrial design in lieu of architecture.
I am anxious to participate in this Anglo-Saxon debate with my Latin and Modern background.

Paul Koralek

Architecture is a process. We are talking about the results of the process, and the classification of the results of the process. It is the manner in which we engage in this process which will determine the results. If we start with the question of style, we are starting from the outside in. But it is the quality of the digestion and the integration, the synthesis or whatever words we use, which finally produces the building. This is surely what we should be concerned with – what goes into the process.

Ted Cullinan

There seems to be quite miserably and definitely a re-understanding, not of the social aspects of Modernism, or of the original Modernism, but very dangerous aspects in which architects tend to think they could actually make up happiness or goodness. Not the town planning aspects of Modernism in which architects tended to flex their imaginary muscles, but the absolute kernel of Modernism which is something that was born before the First World War in Cubism and abstraction. It is not only a very exciting and poignant way to start the practical prose of places and spaces that interpenetrate with one another and are constructed from pieces. But it is a way that none of us can avoid any house

because it is so profoundly in our history and our tradition. I was actually quoting William Morris when he said that tradition is history and the very nature of history is change. In that sense, clearly looking at magazines, at work of other architects and teaching in schools, one does see recently a very strong re-understanding of that part of the tradition of the which is intolerable but fairly understandable. There is nothing we can do about it, except understand it, along with the rest of our inheritance from our past.

Q: If you wanted New Modernists would you teach it?
Architecture today, in the pluralist world of the end of this century, probably offers a more complex mixture of local specificities and worldwide cultural uniformities than at any time in history. Given the mobility of ideas and employment for architects which this represents, the problem of training young people to understand this melee, and cooperate responsibly within it, is of a qualitatively different order form anything that has gone before. In our own teaching, in the upper years of a wide range of architectural schools, we see students struggling within the limitations of their architectural knowledge. They cannot move forward because they have only the most trivial understanding of the principles which architecture has at its disposal today for solving its complex problem. It must be the task of architectural education to train the student to provide this, as something of the status of a basic human right, with whatever resources may be available.

Our students will face even greater rates of change, yet we are not equipping them with any intellectual apparatus at the level of underlying systems, with which they can navigate through that change responsibly and continue to give society real architecture. We see it as precisely the analysis of architectures' fundamentals conducted earlier in the century that can now make it possible to handle today's situation of cultural and philosophical pluralism in a responsible manner, with products of aesthetic, technical and social quality. The last two decades have seen an explosion of historical and critical work on the Modern period in architecture. This explosion has produced material of great detail and sophistication. But from the designer's point of view it has produced a great deal of noise. Neither minute historical research nor higher speculation about relationships between buildings and philosophies is actually teachable to students setting out into architecture. It does not illuminate the design problem faced by the student, and is not usable by the busy professional in search of a design solution at a drawing board.

For half a century, beginning in the 1920s, the following three elements have characterised what we know as the modern world: 1) universalism based on industrialisation; 2) a division of labour based on function; and 3) elimination of classes. Industrial products such as watches, automobiles and aeroplanes were great luxuries when first invented, but our industrial society now provides these things in great quantity and at reasonable prices to the masses, fulfilling its great dream of producing the blessings of a material civilisation and eliminating the gap between rich and poor. As a result, many of us can buy anything from a watch to a personal computer with our pocket money.

This great wave of industrialisation gave birth to the International Style in architecture. This is the Modern architecture we are all so familiar with, the great boxes of steel, glass and concrete.

But this universal model is in fact based on the values and the ethos of Western civilisation. Again, the resemblance to Esperanto is clear, for Esperanto was a universal language based on Western languages. Modernisation turned out to be industrialisation,

Ivor Richards and Catherine Cooke

"Our students will face even greater rates of change . . ."

Kisho Kurokawa

based on the value system of the West; and the developing nations, in their pursuit of modernisation through industrialisation, have all quite naturally pursued Westernisaton with equal keenness.

I must make perfectly clear, however, that in rejecting the universalism and internationalism that presupposed the superiority of the West, I do not advocate a static traditionalism or narrow racialism. I believe instead that the coming age will be a time when the different regions of the world will re-examine their own traditions. On the international level, each region will confront the values and standards of other regions and, while mutually influencing each other, each will produce its own distinctive culture. Rather than internationalism, I call this interculturalism.

I do not totally reject the Modern by any means. My own work always makes use of what I regard as the positive aspects of Modern architecture. But when I see how rigid it has become, how it has lost all flexibility, I am forced to ally myself with those who attack the weaknesses of the Modernist doctrine both of architecture and society. The abstraction of Modernism is a by-product obtained as a result of industrialisation; it is only accidental, and it has ended up as a single-coded – or a completely silent – architecture, lacking as Louis Althusser put it, an epistemology.

"Each building speaks to us . . ."

When we walk through the streets of an Italian Renaissance city – Florence, for example – the experience of just strolling along is highly enjoyable. Each building speaks to us, each sculpture engages us in conversation. We can read the streets, just as we read a novel. The city is a work of literature, and we can browse through it as we walk.

Mood, feeling and atmosphere can each be described as a symbolic order without an established structure. It is through a variety of dynamic, intersecting relationships and juxtapositions – the relationship between one sign and other symbolic elements with which it stands; the way the content of the sign changes when it is quoted; the existence of a medium, an intermediating space introduced between different elements; the relation of the parts to the whole – that mood, feeling and atmosphere are created.

In architecture, the meaning produced by the individual elements placed here and there, and by their relationships, is multivalent and ambiguous. When this meaning creates a feeling and an atmosphere, architecture can approach poetic creation.

To regard architecture as no more than actual space, a stacking of bricks on top of each other, is to accept the models of the pyramid and the tree. But the alternative is to consider all elements of architecture as words (signs), between which new meanings and atmospheres can be created. Since all elements of the work of architecture – the pillars, ceilings, walls, stairways, windows, skylights, rooms enclosed by walls, entrance ways, open spaces, furniture, lighting, door handles, the treatment of the walls – exist as quotations, transformations, sophistications, connotations, symbolisations and intermediations, the solid, substantial architecture, the stack of bricks, is already deconstructed.

Another way of describing the discovery of meaning in the intermediary space between elements is to say that we are evoking meaning by setting elements in relation to each other. Pillars and walls, which have only had meaning as structural elements in architecture up to now, can be deconstructed from the hierarchy of structure and given independent symbolic existence. Differentiation of architecture will be achieved in the evocation of new meanings, bringing differences and variety into new work.

Without a doubt, the architecture of today's informations society will shift from a paradigm of symmetry to asymmetr, from being self-enclosed to being open-ended, form the whole to the part, from structuring to deconstruction and from centrality to

non-centrality, aiming for the freedom and uniqueness of all human beings, for the symbiosis of different cultures, and of a spiritually rich pluralistic society.
Kisho Kurokawa, *Intercultural Architecture – The Philosophy of Symbiosis*

Mark Fisher

I really cannot tell the difference between the arguments of all the people re-examining Modernism. Because it seems to me, from where we are now, that it is all old material. We are not developing any new formal arguments. Within the urban context and given the ubiquitous and straight forward nature of building construction in the late 20th century, you can do what you like as long as the client can pay for it. The concealed importance of capitalism in these conversations and the concealed power of the architect as a persuader, those are the things that shape architecture.

"...you can do what you like as long as the client can pay for it."

Roberto Pirzio Biroli

I think the Modern movement wants to integrate the suburban communities giving them urban centrality. The New Moderns claim to be the interpreters of a continuous acceleration of modernity which does not tolerate rigid and standardised urban architectural projects but explores new concepts, techniques, formal languages and ties between architecture, society, development and survival of identity and values.
New Modernism can only be revolutionary and conservative, a kind of bridge between disarticulation of the city and its recentralisation. The New Modernists have to courageously outline the permanent conflict between the new rationality of the calculating man and the unexpected accidentality of the thinking man.

John Melvin

The new Moderns can be divided into three groups: 1. The Whites 2. The Instrumentalists 3. The Expressionists. The Whites take the forms of heroic Modernism and attempt to give them the kiss of life with new technology. Conran has been doing this with household objects successfully for 20 years, playing upon our sense of nostalgia and our desire to return to a lost age of innocence (when the grain silos were white). However much these forms may have mimicked the machine, they were in essence derived from Cubist paintings and carried a burden of meaning that was a product of a particular time and place in 20th-century art. It is sentiment at best and kitsch at worst to repeat the forms that have outrun their original supporting idea, however much they hold out a bogus consolation of sanitised abstraction to an otherwise intricate and often conflicting world.

The Instrumentalists, like the Whites, adopt familiar 19th-century industrial forms, made familiar to us by Constructivism, to provide metaphors without meaning. They promise to organise our world in accordance with some technical theory where all is reduced to lines, points and grids. Here man is given no concept of himself except as a mere inconvenience and intruder into a scientistic Utopia.

The Expressionist view of the world is from the first person singular with stimulated emotional outbursts that are completely self-directed and opaque to any public participation.

These are all revivals which are primarily stylistic, distanced from the germ of life, or from any indication of a human world or moral order. They are merely academic. Their natural habitat is the museum. It is not surprising therefore that their authors should find favour among curators, their architecture being one more exhibit on display in the counterfeit currency of modern museum art.

The New Modernism is the main design direction in architecture today. In the

Peter Pran

universities in New York, I would say 99 percent of all students are doing what architects call the New Modern architecture. It is rich, strong and authentic architecture that expresses itself in a tremendous range of creativity. It is a new Modern architecture that could not exist without the work of Le Corbusier and Mies van der Rohe, but it is also substantially different from what they created. It does not repeat the Modern architecture of the previous two decades but extends it. Furthermore, the new Modern architecture does not return to the so-called pragmatic, uncreative and boring commercial box buildings, that unfairly discredited Modern architecture, and led some to escape into Post-Modern historicism. These deadly commercial buildings were mistakenly perceived as an end to Modern design.

Post-Modernism today clearly means historicism and revivalism through the superficial and nostalgic copying of older buildings and styles. Historicism is antithetical to our own culture; it shows a lack of belief in our own time, in our technology and in our own creative strength. When we reverse time and go back into history for copying purposes, we undermine society's ability to create our own authentic culture and create important buildings which are representative of our own epoch.

The contemporary city should reject the nostalgic, classical, Post-Modern so-called 'contextual' urban design with its enormous potential for invention and elaboration. By going forward, by creating a new Modern architecture, one is exploring new aspects of what it means to be a human being living in the contemporary city; through an honest and invigorating exploration, one is seeking new insight. Architecture is the principal means of urban transformation.

Peter Wilson

England and, to a large extent America, are today's architectural backwaters: it is only there that the question 'Does a new Modernism exist' is asked. Elsewhere, what Branzi has called 'The Second Modernism' is well underway. It is not a revival or play with forms of 'Heroic Modernism'. It is architecture consequent to today's technological and perceptual revolution, an architecture of clear unmannered forms which accept and give measure to the discontinuous post-industrial field.

Claudio Silvestrin

Architecture as nourishing thought for grounding our being on the earth has been lost for some time. This decline does not result only from the fact that the quality is poorer and the style less imposing; it is rather that architecture forfeits its original essence of representing the absolute. Individual and exceptional works that exist only for the enjoyment of a few sectors of the population do not speak against the assertion that architecture as 'orientation' has lost its historical power and survives only as a discourse.

Yet today as never before architectural discourse stubbornly persists within its own self and it is precisely from the possibility of its own death that architecture can be interrogated in such countless numbers of books, fashions, styles, photographs, images and words. Even the question 'What is Architecture' inhabits such dwarfed discourse and finding the correct assertion does not matter since the question already leads towards the assumption that architecture would be predetermined or precomprehended in it as an object in which one claims to distinguish an inner meaning.

The whole Utopia of Modernism has claimed a return of the absolute by means of science and technology. Yet technology tries in vain to make function what is not functioning. Le Corbusier, Mies and Fuller (to name a few) were part of such a belief. They interpreted the unity art/science as handsome technology. Are the 'New Moderns' (by implication from their label) following the belief of their masters?

"Architecture is the principal means of urban transformation."

The Modernists of the 80s fulfil the re-emergence of a Modernist aesthetic in contemporary architectural discourse but only within its own discourse and only as aesthetic or, to be more precise, as style.

I fear that, fundamentally, the New Moderns are still trapped in Modern thought – that is technological thought – thus going side by side with the non-Moderns. Now that the century is ending in fear, it may be time to direct our creative energy in questioning the beliefs of Modernity.

Because of the constantly accelerating pace of the contemporary business environment, design professionals today tend to rely more than ever upon publications in their field for information about current trends. The plurality that has now come to characterise the international architectural scene makes reliance upon the media even more necessary for practitioners and students alike, who continue to seek a barometer by which they can gauge the impact of each new change upon their work. When a consensus finally does emerge, the media serves not only to report such changes, but also guides and magnifies them, becoming a formidable force in its own right. Instead of presenting an extensive litany of either the recently commissioned or completed examples of New Modern architecture, it should suffice to merely mention that such a consensus has now been reached in the media, and that this tectonic direction is undeniably alive and well. Based on the number of awards given to Modernist buildings in the January 1990 issue of the American publication *Progressive Architecture*, and the countless features on individual buildings that have appeared in magazines and journals during the last year, as well as the recent publication of *The New Moderns* there appears to be overwhelming evidence that this much maligned style has now been reborn, if indeed it ever died at all.

This regrettable rebirth is a poignant reminder of the wisdom inherent in the French phrase 'plus ça change, plus c'est la même chose'. In a benchmark article by Robert Venturi, published in *Architectural Record* eight years ago, this perceptive architect used the same phrase as a title and went on precisely to identify the fatal flaw of the movement which many then thought would offer salvation from the strictures of Modernist doctrine. 'Post-modernism,' he said then 'has proclaimed in theory its independence from Modernism, from the singular vocabulary and the rigid ideology of that movement, but has substituted, in practice, a new vocabulary that is different in its symbolism from the old, but similar in its singularity and as limited in its range and dogmatic in its principles as the old. In this respect it is not different from the previous movement.'

In retrospect, the recent resurrection of Modernism appears to be nothing more than a lock-step sequel to that failure. Following as closely behind Post-Modernism and Deconstructivism as it does, the latest stage in this cycle seems like a replay of a previous scenario that resulted in the International Style itself. All of the players are there, complete with Post-Modernism in the role of resurgent tradition; Deconstructivism filling in for the Constructivism that followed it, but without a social mandate, and the New Modernism as the rehabilitated star, striving once again to express 'the Technology of the times', but not the will of the people.

Can those who ascribe to this direction seriously expect others to simply overlook the sterile legacy of its predecessor, or believe that a few superficial, stylistic gestures can justify a return to the elitist attitudes of the past? Such attitudes have not previously been receptive to social needs and aspirations, and there is no reason to believe that they will do so in the future.

James Steele

". . . much maligned style has now been reborn . . ."

Serves you right! say I as an architectural traditionalist. For a generation Modern architects have been tearing up what little civic order and morality that remained in Modern architecture in proliferating a Babel of architectural styles. 'The impersonal spirit of Bach', as Le Corbusier once put it, went out; showbiz originality came in. Robert Venturi had asked that Modern architects make Las Vegas their Florence; yes, Las Vegas where each building becomes a billboard shouting for attention. They did as bidden. Lo, the Babel of Las Vegas came to pass: in La Défense, in the Docklands, in Athens, in Fort Lauderdale, indeed everywhere that a post-sixties Modern architecture was given head. And now, with perfect justice, Babel has come to roost even among its priests who cannot even figure out a common terminology, not less a protocol for governing an argument.

Consider the question of what name should be applied to the bright new thing in Modern architecture. 'Late', it would seem, came too early; handy when it distinguished Magpie Moderns who quoted historical styles from Lego-Loyalists who didn't; yet hopeless when it had to embrace not just an I M Pei or a Richard Rogers, but a Peter Eisenman who exploded the Lego-set into warped walls, rootless rafters, broken axes and smashed corners.

'Post', it would seem, ran into problems of copyright: it was all very well for an Eisenman or a Tschumi to try on the title of 'Post' in claiming that their 'Post' was pitched further on from old-style Lego-like Modern architecture than the 'Post' of Charles Jencks. A more technical name such as Deconstructionist Architecture (or should it be Deconstructivist ?), it would appear, suffered for being not too general but too exact – or, more exactly, too exactly general : the legitimate complaint against it (that is, aside from the fact that deconstruction is both a critical method and a relativist philosophy) is that it would turn an argument about quoting or not quoting into a bun fight between Tweedle-Dee and Tweedle-Dum. Both schools already admit to sharing the central doctrine of Multivalence. The word 'Deconstruction' would only slam the point home in underscoring an awkward truth: that Multivalence makes more sense as part of a larger relativist philosophy of Deconstruction that argues that multiple readings arise from the arbitrary and non-referential nature of the sign. But if both schools share the same central doctrine and underlying philosophy why should it matter if one quotes and the other doesn't? Quoting or not quoting are matters of indifference in contemporary modern music. Why shouldn't quoting or not quoting be matters of indifference in contemporary Modern architecture as well?

By a process of elimination, then, we are stuck with the name actually chosen: *New*. No one can really complain if only because no one can be really sure what the word *New* is supposed to mean. Certainly a traditionalist like me isn't going to kick up a fuss. How can I about a name that has enforced obsolescence built into it and is already redolent of *déja vu*? Make it New, demanded Ezra Pound – and Modern architects made it just that, with streets in the air and gymnasia on the roof and crèches on the ground – and always in the name of a new Minerva that slipped inadvertently from their thigh, never in the name of newness for its own sake or the career opportunities that newness opened up for tooting their own horn.

We have seen some odd architectural Minervas in our time. Only think of those Minervas celebrating the motor-car that rode through Modern architecture like the proud nose piece of a Rolls Royce, now telling us to push motorways through the centre of our cities, now demanding that, like Santa Claus, motorways should ride over the rooftops, now insisting that we even remake our buildings into road signs so as to be more in scale and entertaining for motorists. Yet, as odd as Minervas go, this latest must

" . . .what name should be given to the bright new thing in Modern Architecture."

"We have seen some odd Architectural Minervas in our time."

take the cake. For what is this new certainty? It is a certainty about uncertainty, nay, it is an absolute certainty about absolute uncertainty.

Even on the first meeting this new Minerva exudes the bad breath of *mauvaise foi* in pretending to be more uncertain than she really is. Indeed, she is playing a sly game of self-contradiction in her certainty about uncertainty of a kind that Epimenidas pinned down in the 6th century BC: if all Cretans are liars is not he as a Cretan telling the truth? Now what is dangerous in a self-contradictory game about uncertainty is that, in practising a secret *superbia cognoscendi*, it all but invites self-certainty through the back door. For Heidegger self-certainty was the Nazi Party. For Paul de Man it was anti-Semitism. And for Eisenman self-certainty is simply *chutzpah* when he tells us that he has stood before the Parthenon and Ronchamps and found them both lacking the all-vital Presence that is nowadays to be found in the uncertainties of a New Modern Architecture. But how can he be so certain? And how can he speak so freely of Presence when Presence, as Derrida has argued, is unknowable in a Deconstructionist philosophy?

But there is something far stranger in this new Minerva than the hidden *chutzpah* of her self-certainty: she seems hell-bent on making monkeys of her own acolytes in turning the whole argument into a Deconstructionist exercise which reverses the conclusion from the one intended. The change-about happens in the switch from private literary readings to a public act. As the art that, willy nilly, we foist upon our neighbour, architecture will always prompt a civic question about the architect's own authority. So when a New Modern Architect, Frank Gehry, asks why not fish as a signifier rather than a Corinthian capital, the civic response will be to hear the question, not as rhetorical, but as offering an actual choice. If one signifier is ultimately as arbitrary as another, why can't the public have a reverberant signifier that it already knows?

To be sure, an Eisenman challenges civic authority with the authority of the architect as a Nietzchean Superman who is duty-bound to bring the 'unrepression', as Eisenman puts it, of architectural form. But we in civic society know how to handle architectural Supermen, be they architects or otherwise. They can make out a planning application like the rest of us and 'unrepress' architectural form before the building work.

How sad for the New Modern Architects! Given the discipline of a public participation, their very arguments would no doubt frog-march them back to traditional forms of architecture that the Old Modern Architecture had already overthrown. And why not? For what do the New Modern Architects offer but intellectual encouragement to the Babel of discourses and modern styles we have had too much of already? That frog-march, too, would serve them right!

ODILE DECQ & BENOIT CORNETTE
THE MODEL IS THE MESSAGE & BANQUE POPULAIRE DE L'OUEST RENNES

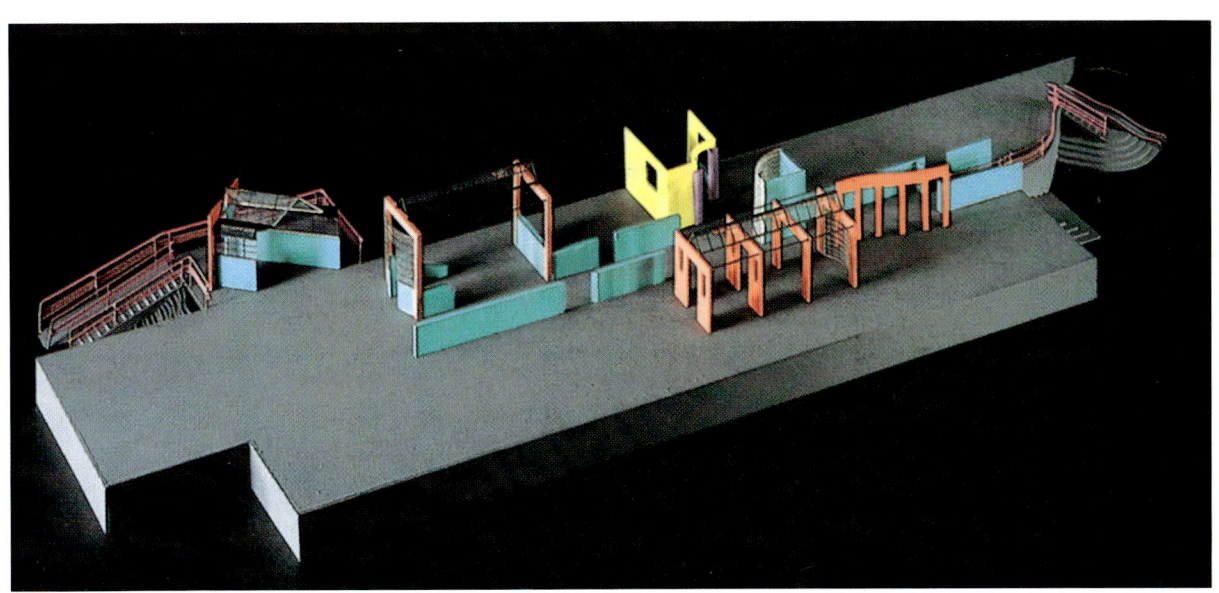

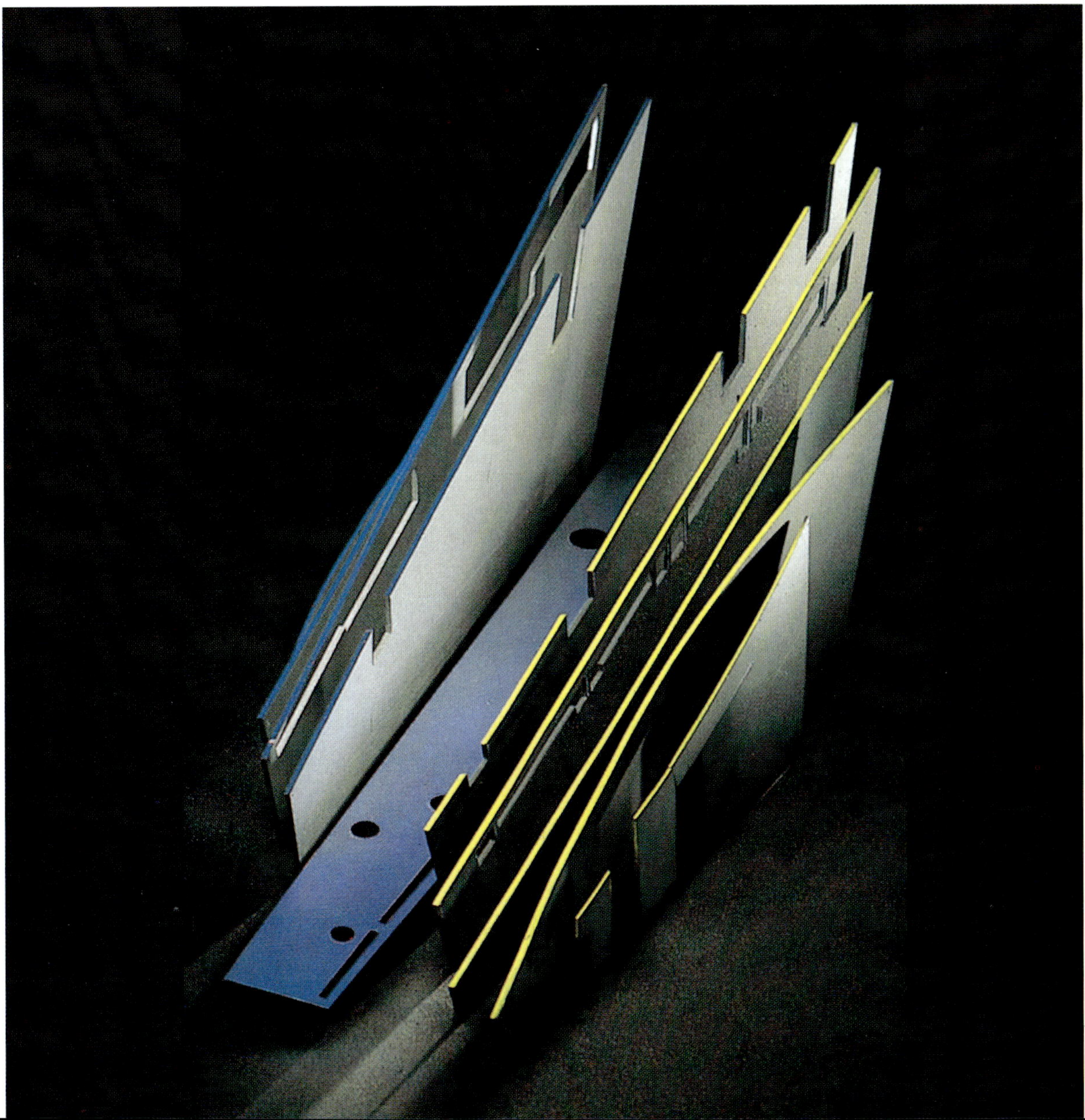

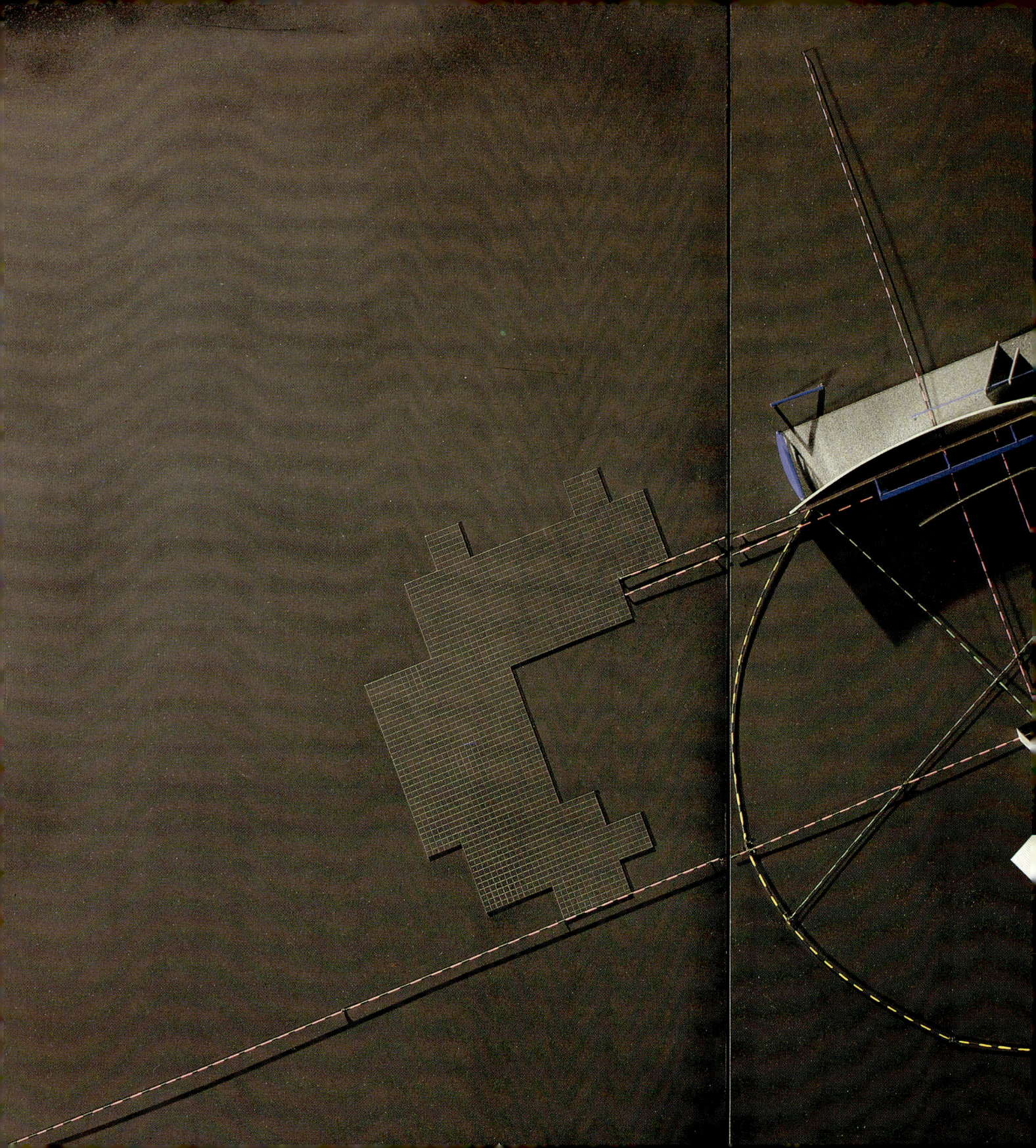

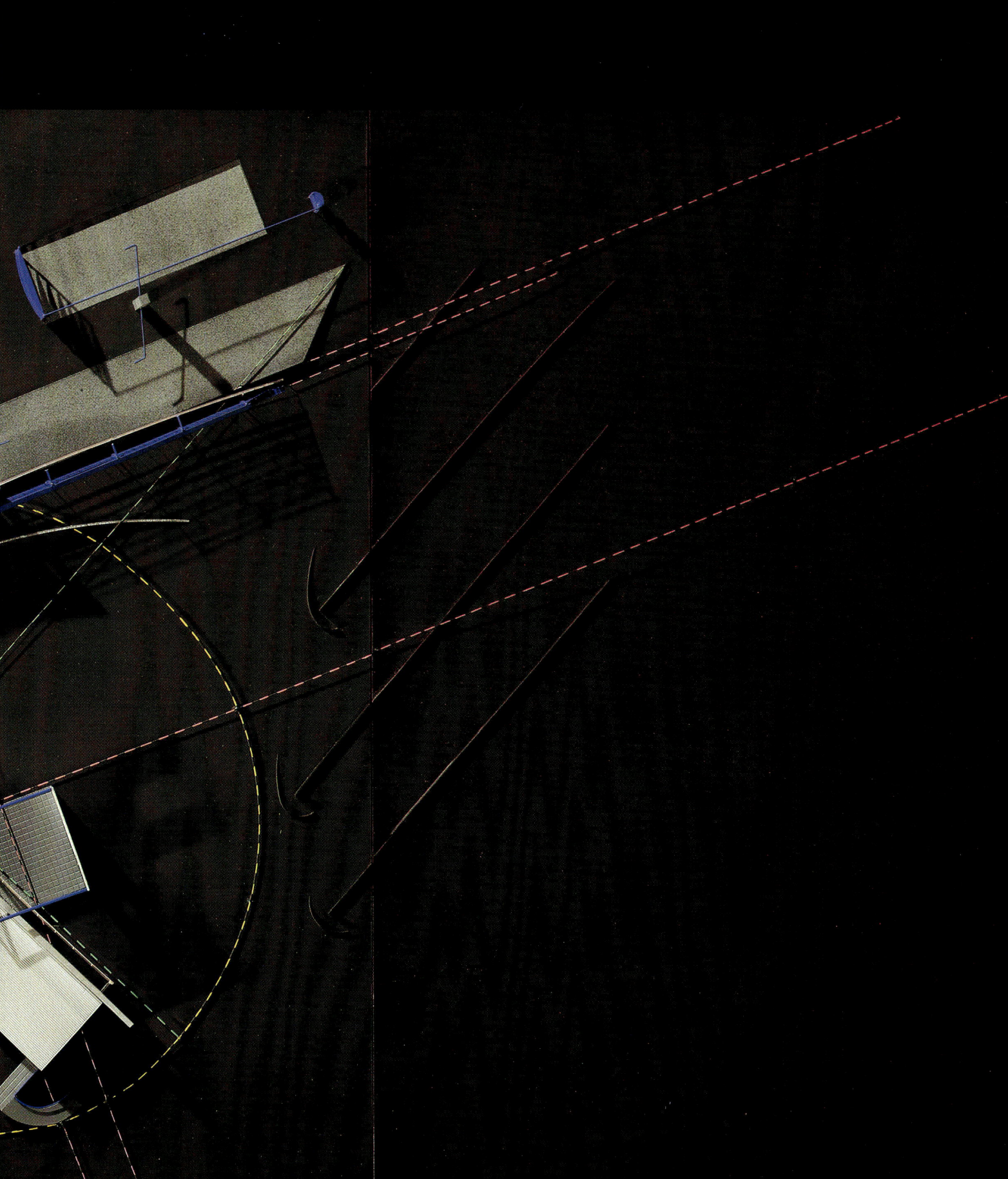

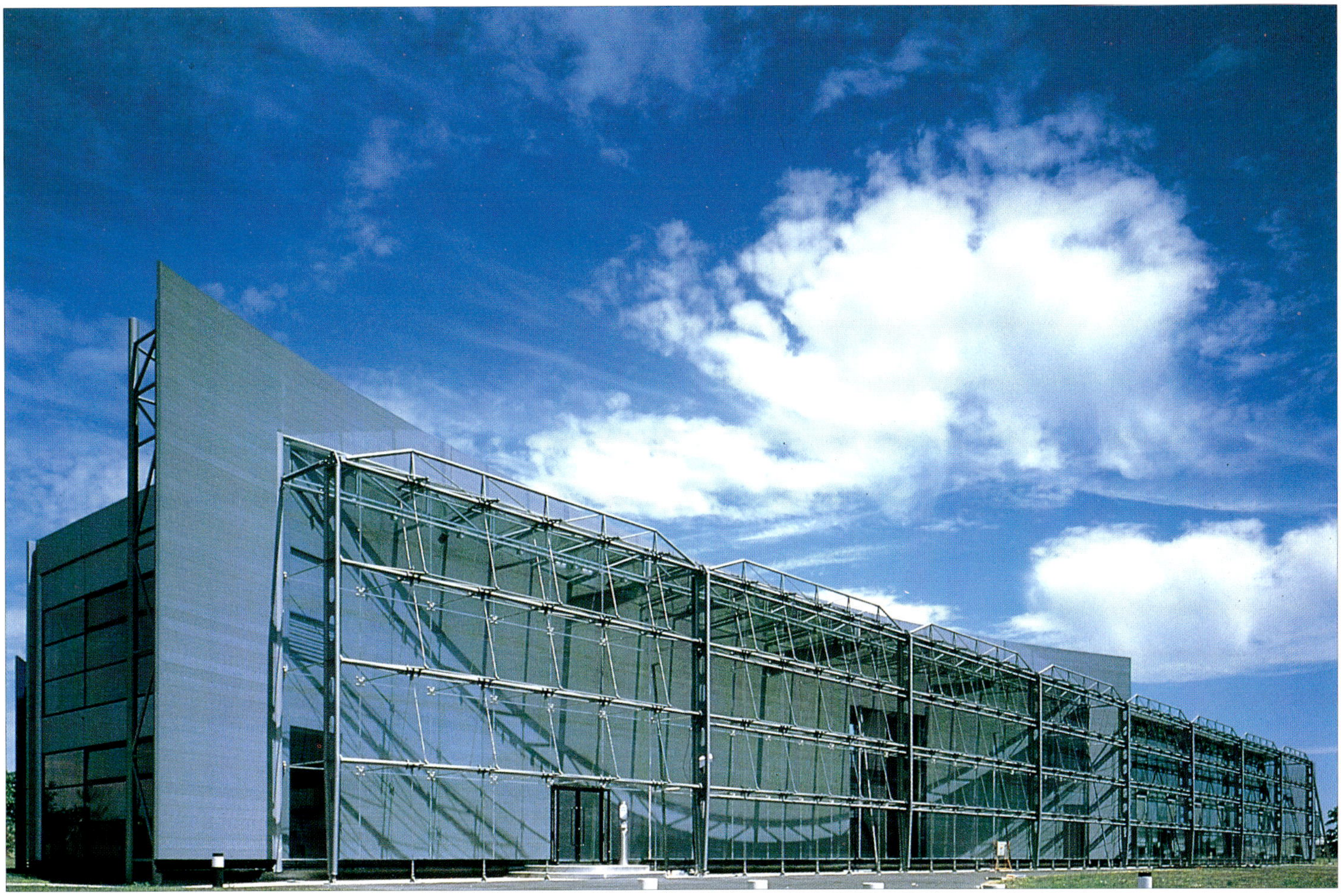

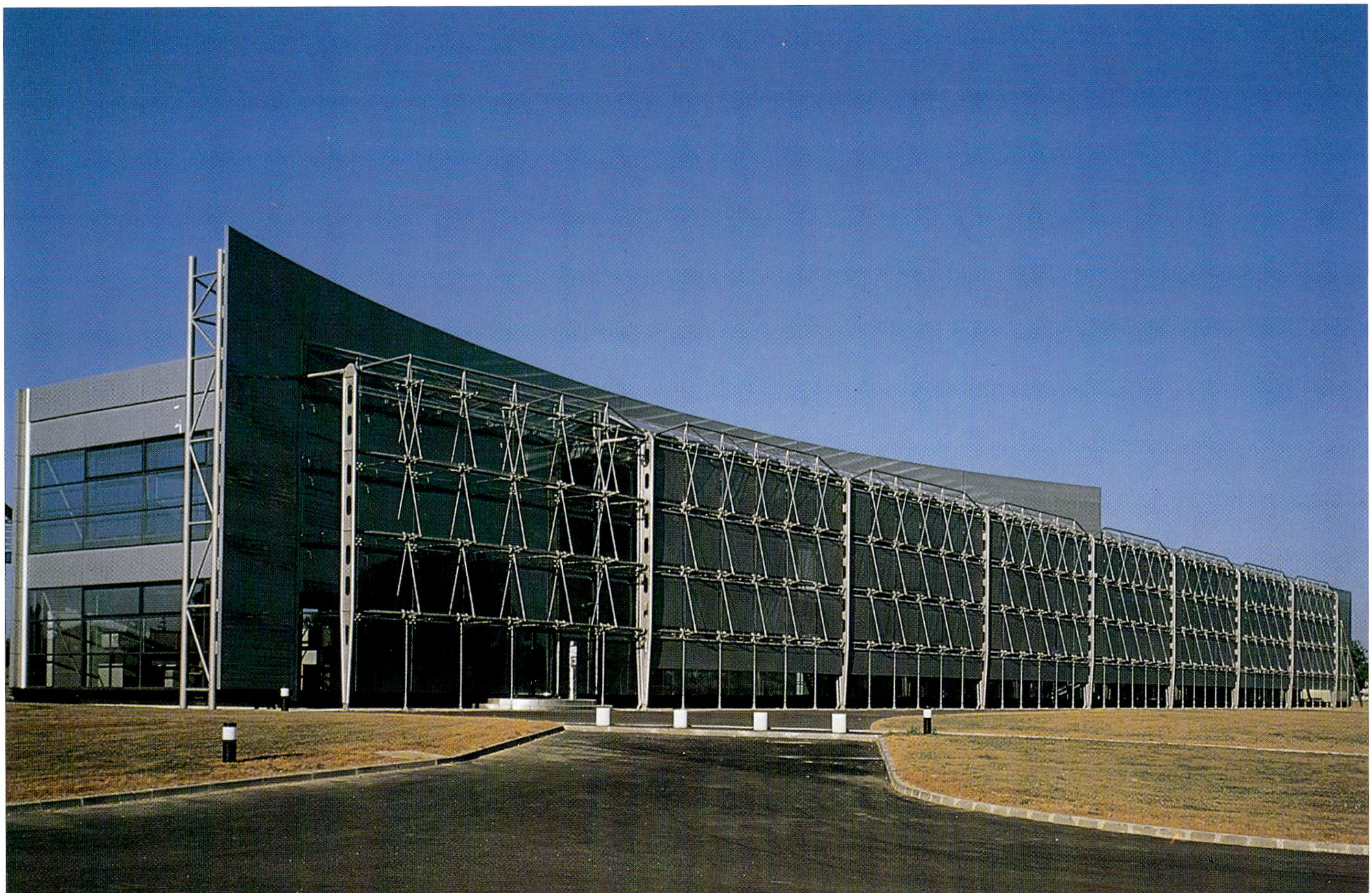

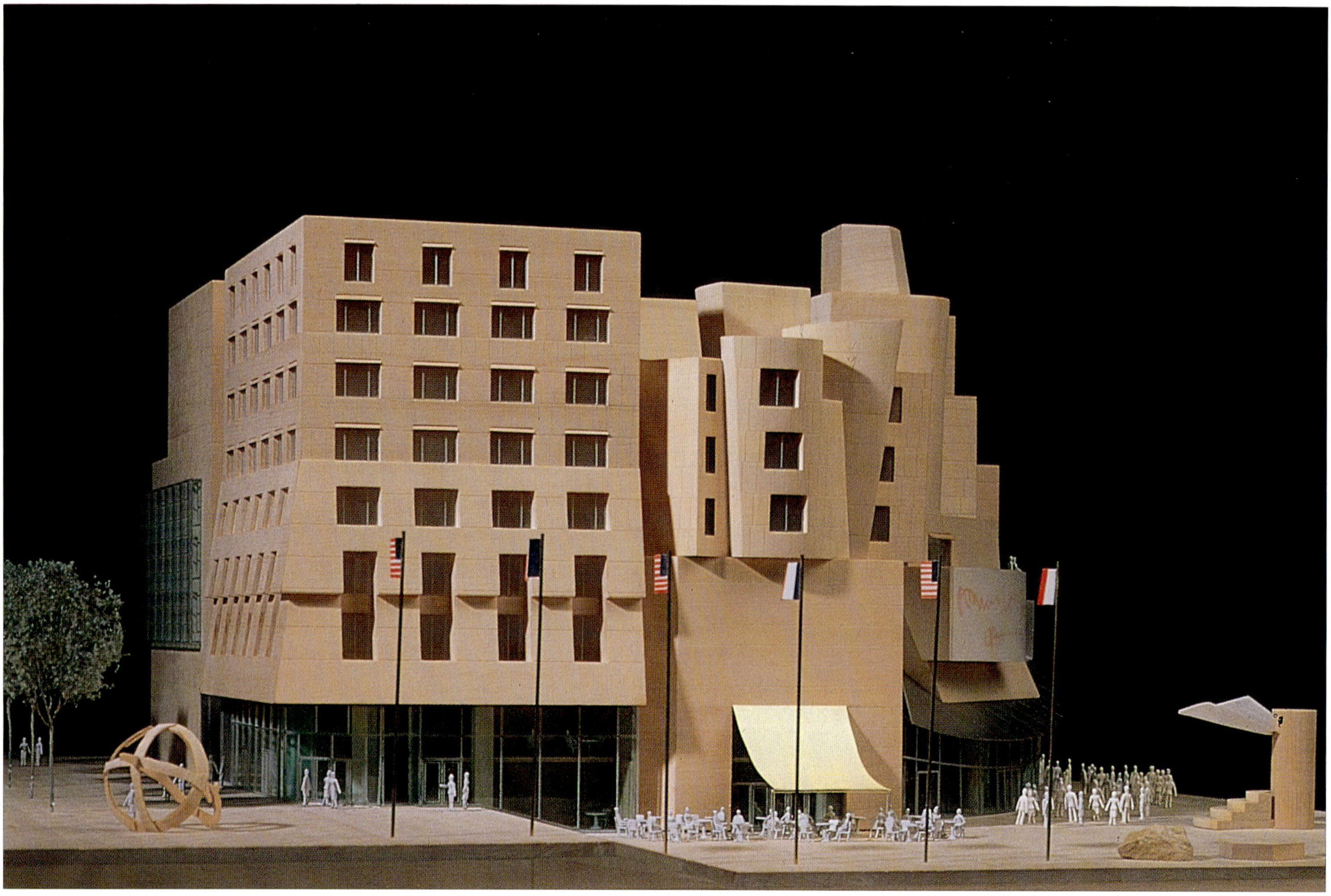

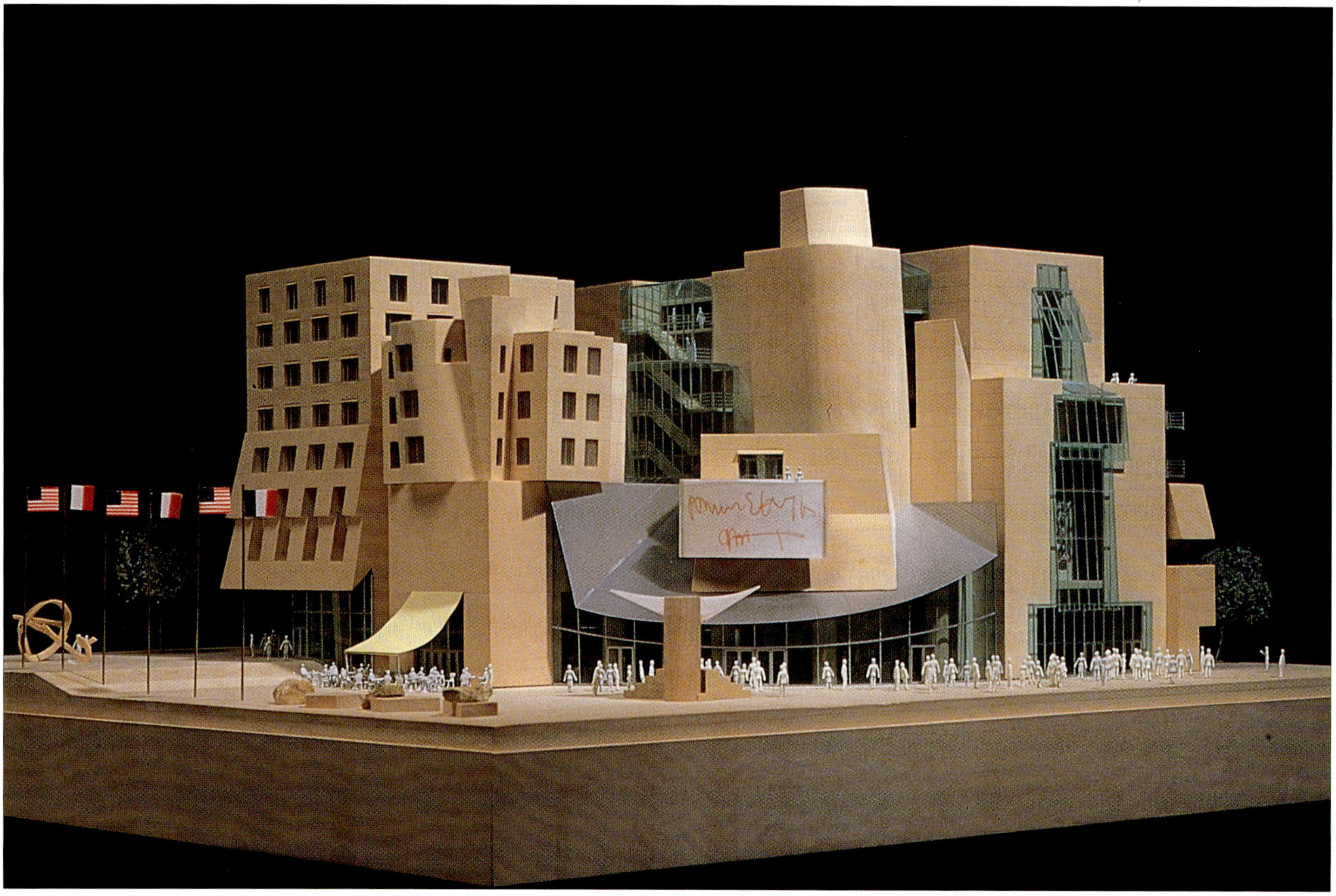

FRANK GEHRY

THE AMERICAN CENTER IN PARIS

– What has the American Center commission meant for you?
This is the first full-fledged cultural institution dealing with the arts as a permanent building that I have done outside of America. It's a very important project for me. I've worked with cultural institutions in the States. I did buildings for the Temporary Contemporary [an auxiliary facility of The Museum of Contemporary Art in Los Angeles], the California Aerospace Museum, the Goldwyn Library [in Los Angeles], the Cabrillo Marine Museum. For me, as someone very involved with sculpture and art and dance and music – those things are part of my life, I take my nourishment from them – to be offered a project like the American Center has been very exciting. The fact that it was in France gave it an extra boost. The Europeans are just now getting a new slant on American architecture. There have been some commercial buildings done there recently by Americans, and then of course Pei's Pyramid. So this project is very important to me and I have invested a lot of my gut in the American Center.
– Is this your first project in France?
It is the first project to be built in France. And I think there is a healthy scepticism among the French architects here regarding this project. You know they would have preferred a French architect to do it even though it's an American center. Especially after the Pei Pyramid. I have to say though that, so far, the agencies we've been working with – the French building department and planning departments and all of the people we've met with to explain the project and approve the various parts – have been very, very receptive. It's exciting especially because in France, these people are particularly knowledgeable about art and architecture, which is very, very different from the kind of character you find in America. The French in those capacities are a lot more cultured.
– How familiar were you with Paris before this project?
Well, I lived and worked there in an architecture firm in 1960 and I've never forgotten the energy. It's something to draw from. I like it. Paris is a very intense city. Lots of people, lots of traffic. I have always been intrigued with France. It's a feisty society. It's not laid back. It's cranky and has an edge to it. They don't accept foreigners easily, either. It's a fascinating society to me. I like the French because they are quick to the point. They don't try to cover everything up. I want the American Center building to be just like Paris. It will be a city, a *petit ville*, full of dance and music and activity and a lot of energy like the city.
– Is it safe to say, then, that you are creating a very French building for the American Center?
Not really. The building is like the institution; it's about two perspectives, European and American. It's an American's interpretation of Paris as I see it, without trying to make a French building. I tried to deal with the mixture of cultures. It's a kind of "American in Paris." I see the building as very Parisian and very American. And also as very festive because that's what it's about.
– Could this building exist in California?
To me, France is about street life. A particular type of street life which couldn't exist in Los Angeles. I made a street life building for Paris which couldn't exist in Los Angeles. You couldn't put this building there. It's about context and the French context involves certain traditions and conventions. At the same time,

the building is also very unconventional. That is, you walk up to the building and you think it's conventional at first, but then you'll blink.
– Could you explain how some of the actual details of the building create that effect of being both American and European? What did you do to make the transition from the conventional to the unconventional in one structure?
Well, if you look at the model and the plans for the building you can understand it better. You see the Rue Bercy? It's on the north side of the building. That is the way one arrives at the American Center building coming down the street from the Metro. You come down the street and the first image you get of the building is this facade on the north side that is, for me, anyway, especially simple, comfortable, polite to the street and the existing surroundings. It has a calm facade and it breaks down into two masses on that side that respond to the scale of the buildings on that street. I've done a sort of classic mansard here, but I made the mansard slip down the side of the building, down to the ground. At the ground floor, there are glass store fronts like the ones in other buildings on the street. So from the beginning you think you have a discreet building. But as you move around the site it changes.
– In what way?
Well, as you come around the building from the street side you enter Bercy Park, the main axis toward the Seine, and the building starts to become more sculptural. The first thing you encounter on this side of the building, the west side, is a small sidewalk cafe that belongs to the Center. And above it, where you see a blank wall on the facade, is a 100-seat cinema. And the more articulated piece on top of that is what I call "the pineapple." There are three special apartments there that are part of the housing. They look out on the park. I wanted these to be very special. The forms here start to get a little, you know, different, a little unexpected, more animated. So then you move around the building from the pineapple into the park and you find the entrance to the building, where the building just explodes into a kind of exuberant form so that it is perceived as a kind of actual sculptured piece in the landscape of the Bercy Park. It's joyous, friendly, happy, welcoming. We put all the animation on the park side and it's very unconventional, very American. It's very energetic and very, very three dimensional.
– There are all kinds of unusual volumetric pieces over and above the entrance to the building. They are sort of massed together. And they do look, to use your word, sculptural. Can you elaborate on these forms? Where did they come from?
Well, when I'm working I consider context. And the Parisian context is stone and metal roofs, very sculptural roofs. If you look at the Hotel de Ville, the sculptural character of that building is very strong. It's got the best cleavage in Paris. Its big, V-shaped spaces and the articulation between the roofs and fireplaces make a strong statement. For me that is the best of Paris.
– You've often been quoted as saying that your architecture is informed by painting and sculpture, causing some to think of you more as an artist than an architect.
I am an architect. I do think that art and architecture come from the same source. They involve some of the same struggles. My

first work, when I started to do my own stuff, was encouraged by artists, not by other architects. Actually, other architects were suspicious of my work. Ed Ruscha, Ed Moses, the Los Angeles artists have always been very, very supportive. They became my support system and they are still my support system today. I am a product of the sixties. People like Ruscha, Richard Serra, Claes Oldenburg, Carl Andre – they came out of the same time, the same mentality. I have always been interested in their work. I always related to their thinking and to the expressions of that time – minimalism, pop art. I relate to these guys. In a lot of ways we are very similar, but I'm an architect.

– *Where are the similarities?*

I came to architecture through fine arts and painting is still a fascination for me. Paintings are a way of training the eye. You see how people compose a canvas. The way Bruegel composes a canvas versus the way Caravaggio composes a canvas or Jasper Johns. I learned about composition from their canvases. I picked up all those visual connections and ideas. And I find myself using them sometimes. The ideas of space through paintings, through the Pinturicchio paintings in Siena which are just beautiful, huge, spatial experiences. They are about cities. And Lorenzetti, Gentile Bellini, Carpaccio. All of these paintings are about space and cities. Piet Mondrian has inspired the window and wall elevations of many buildings from Gropius to Corbusier. I have been fortunate to have had support from living painters and sculptors. I have never felt that what artists are doing and architects are doing is very different. I've always felt there is a moment of truth when you decide what colour, what size, what composition. How you get to that moment of truth is different and the end result is different.

– *Another important aspect of the American Center building is the two masses you mentioned before. These actually house two distinct functions – the cultural center and a housing area. These two masses seem to have a noticeable tension.*

Yeah, they do. At the time the client was asking me to do this building I was thinking of buildings in terms of bottles. You put them together and there's an energy that you don't get from a bottle alone. They have an effect on each other. There's a difference between one bottle alone and six together or even two together. And a building – the parts of a building – should have that energy of bottles, forms together that have an effect on each other.

– *Did you say bottles or bodies?*

I said bottles, but, now that you mention it, I could have said bodies because it's the same thing with bodies. In fact, I didn't originally contrive it this way, but the building is like a ballet dancer, a ballerina lifting her skirt, inviting people to come inside. The entrance, the way it sweeps across, is like the lifted skirt, and the circulation portion where the elevator is – the part that rises over the skirt – is like the figure. The ballerina lifts her skirt up and, since I'm a dirty old man, that's the way you enter the building! I also think of the building as being like a big welcome mat at the entrance to the park. It's open and invites you in.

– *Is that a critical aspect of the building for you – the open, inviting quality?*

Yes. I think the most important thing about the building for me is this idea I have about accessibility. The building has a body language that says "come in", like at the Temporary Contemporary or Disney Hall [a project in the design stage for the Music Center in Los Angeles]. The architecture doesn't get in the way of people walking in and out. It's inviting. The feeling of accessibility is a big priority in all of my work. The key issue for me is, What does the building say to the people on the street, how does it welcome them? And I don't think that destroys or negates an artist's position. I want people to be able to interact with my ideas and not be intimidated by them. This is very important, particularly today. It's what I'm doing with the Disney Hall in Los Angeles. With the American Center building, you feel an easy transition into the building without any intimidation, without feeling that somebody's going to stop you or ask you questions. My architectural language may feel strange to some people. But they should still feel comfortable in my buildings. That's the way the American Center will be, I think. You should see the entrance from the park and feel like coming in, taking your jacket off. I want the building to be like a party in the park, very inviting.

– *Is the park entrance your favourite part of the building?*

Well, it was definitely the toughest part to do.

– *Why was it so difficult?*

We had to conform to certain requirements determined by the city [of Paris] and that involved a chopped off corner on the site, which is called the pan coupe. There's an existing building already to the west of ours which has this cut off corner and we had to promise the city that we'd do the same thing on ours. So the site itself was the greatest challenge. You essentially have

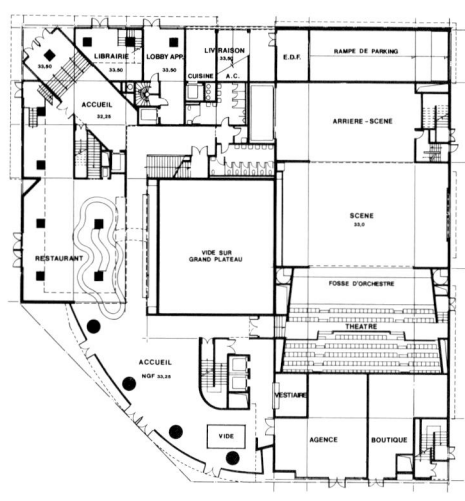

GROUND LEVEL
REZ-DE-CHAUSSÉE

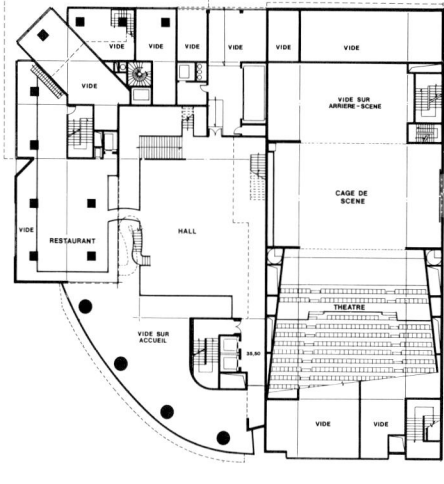

PLATFORM LEVEL
PLATE-FORME

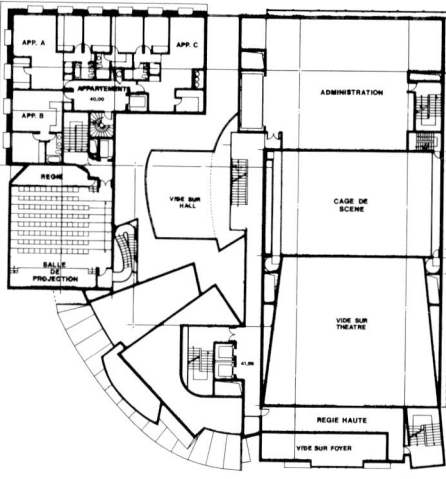

LEVEL +2
NIVEAU +2

this 166 by 170 foot rectangular plot of land with a 66 by 66 foot triangle removed from the southwest corner of the site. I have never had an experience with this before. The pan coupe was a major torture.

– Why?

It meant working with a site that was confining. We had to work with the pan coupe, which is not the way I would usually work, which is about a less controlled, more immediate response to the site.

– How did you cope with the pan coupe in the end?

It was very difficult. First of all we put the main entrance there. If you look in straight elevation at our building, you can see that there's one element, then a second, and then the shaft of the elevator, which is orthogonal. So you have these three pieces in relation to the facade. Then in the front elevation to the park, which is on a diagonal, you have also orthogonally this sculptural element and again this side of the elevator and this side of the apartments. So there again you have the three elements.

The solution to the question of the pan coupe for me, which seems very simple now but took me months to figure out, was to rotate the circulation piece – the elevator shaft, which I call "the leaning tower" – over the entrance on the diagonal to make the transition around the pan coupe. It's complicated. But on each elevation, the pieces are frontal. So there are three parts on each elevation that are frontal, with the elevator tower being frontal in both directions. Then the skirt of the elevator tower – the skirt of the ballerina that I referred to before, which is an awning over the entrance – and this piece with the balcony that sits on top of the entrance roof rotate on the diagonal so that they face the diagonal created by the pan coupe. In fact, I'm always trying to recapture the missing point of the pan coupe. It's wishful thinking I guess. So you see on the model this little structure out in the plaza in front of the Center's entrance. It's a bandstand in the park. That's the missing point of the pan coupe

– What will the visitor encounter at the entrance to the Center?

Well, first of all, my one California act here, or maybe it's a California act, is I hope to be able to have the wide glass doors of the entrance slide all the way back in warm weather so that the entrance is entirely open and the line between inside the Center and outside in the park disintegrates. The leaning tower over the entrance, as I said before, is the vertical circulation, the elevator that leads up to the other levels, and the stairways that surround that. The sculpture of the outside continues on the inside because you have the accueil.

– What is the accueil?

It's a kind of welcoming entry, an atrium on two levels. You can enter the building from the corner out on the Rue Bercy, or from the main entrance on the pan coupe. Either way when you come in you're in the accueil. On the lower level of the accueil, you can go into the restaurant, the bar, the retail shops, the libraries. On the second level of the acceuil – the mezzanine, which is a raised section – you go up and actually engage in the activities of the American Center. This mezzanine is connected to the restaurant also, but it's where you buy tickets and get information and have access to the elevator to go up to the theatre and classes and the rest. The mezzanine can be used for special activities and parties, but also special exhibitions and activities we haven't even thought up yet. These two accueil spaces are different from each other. The lower level space has a small skylight that is related to the stairways and the elevators, but it is essentially covered. And the raised section of the mezzanine has a glass roof. From the mezzanine looking up you will see the sculptural parts of the building very clearly so that the energy of the exterior of the building will inform and be part of the mezzanine and the interior. I really like this part especially – the activity, the animation visible by looking up through the glass skylights.

– That glass part where you can see all the people circulating is reminiscent of the Beaubourg [The Centre Georges Pompidou in Paris]. Was the Beaubourg at all an influence on your design choices here?

I like a lot of things about Beaubourg. But one thing I like especially about it is the feeling of people being all over it, the activity of it being a building inhabited by people. You feel its activity from the outside. At the American Center, we wanted to have balconies and places on the building where you could see people from the outside as well as the courtyard, the stairway, so that it would be animated and its activities would be visible. The energy is important because the Center's program is very charged and intense and dense and it was important that the building reflect the energy of that. The activities which will take place inside the building complement the forms, which are dense, too.

– What do you mean by dense?

The American Center's program is extensive. It's multidisciplinary. Movies and theatre, classes, eating, exhibitions, shopping, people living in apartments. The building has to say what's in it. It

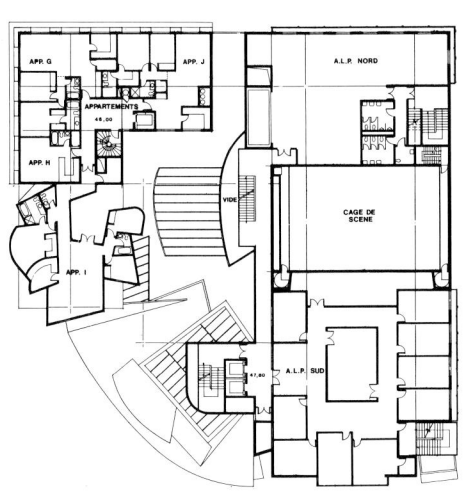

LEVEL +4
NIVEAU +4

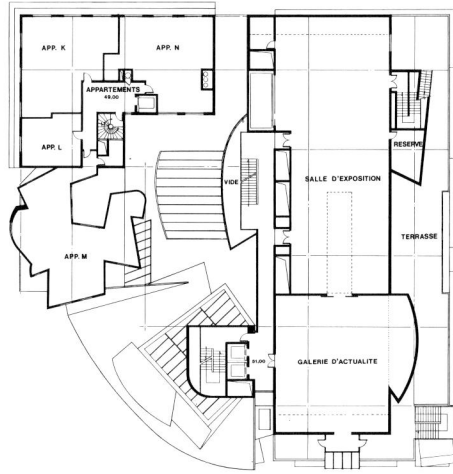

LEVEL +5
NIVEAU +5

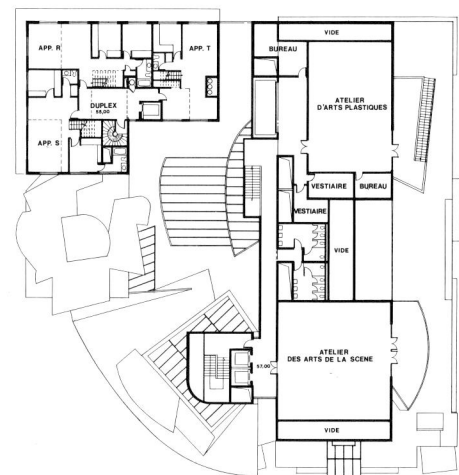

LEVEL +7
NIVEAU +7

has all kinds of uses and functions. There will be circulation in the building at all hours, and that made it complicated to work out. The codes for housing are different from those of the theatre, the restaurant, the museum and so forth. It's like a Swiss watch. I think we've achieved a nice balance. All the forms have been resolved with the density and we still have a humane building.

– Can you tell me more about the details of the building? You left off with an explanation of the entrance.

On the ground floor facing the park on the south side of the building there will be a bookstore which can also be, in summer, I hope, open with outdoor stands full of books and stuff. On the next floor above that there's a large window – in the model through this window you can see we put a Frank Stella – where there's a foyer for the 350-seat proscenium theatre. So when you come out of the theatre you look out of the window and feel the park below. Above this is the language school floor for the American Language Program. And above that are the exhibition galleries. And then above those are two spaces – studios for art and dance classes and rehearsals. There is a balcony that is over the entrance, and people from the gallery can walk around the balcony and have views of the park.

– Why was the dance studio placed over the exhibition galleries? One would expect to have the galleries on the building's top level in order to take full advantage of daylight.

We agonized over that one. We wanted to get natural light into the art gallery with a tall skylight. This way, the way that we have it now, direct light doesn't come in but there's a higher space for the light to come in. If the gallery had been above the dance studio space, on the top floor, the window of the skylight would have been at the same level as the roof and you would have had uncontrollable light. I started with the design the other way around when I was first working on it. But as I studied the reality of the program, this way made better sense with the gallery below.

– And what's happening on the eastern side of the building? It seems to become quiet again in comparison with the very animated south side and the entrance. Does that have anything to do with the fact that there will be an apartment house very close to the Center to the east?

The housing site to the east will be built after our project. I've seen the design, the plans for it. Since we started designing first we took that housing project into account. In general, nothing fronts onto that side so that when the housing is built they won't have our institutional areas staring into their apartments. Their building will be approximately the same height as ours – 24 meters as opposed to our 27 meters. There will be a very small street between the two buildings, just for foot traffic really, and so you will never see much of that facade of the American Center except from the corner. It's just going to be a more quiet side. We will probably grow ivy and plants there. We've focused on the corners; the offices and archives of the American Center are on the two floors of that side, and the third floor is the American Language Program, which I already pointed out from the southern facade. And there's also two balconies on this eastern side.

– Henry Pillsbury [Executive Director of the American Center in Paris] seems particularly fond of those balconies. He talks about them with great enthusiasm.

That's because they have a lot to do with his idea about how the Center is going to be used by artists. He's picturing this one balcony off the studios as a place where dancers are going to hang out in their smelly leotards between rehearsals and artists are going to come out of the studios with paint on their pants and use the stairs to carry paintings and sculptures down to the galleries below. And the other balcony is a place where possibly sculpture can be shown.

– What materials have you chosen for the building?

For the interior I don't know yet. For the exterior we will choose a limestone that is indigenous to France. I don't know for sure what the stone will be. I envision a limestone that has some pink in it.

– And what about other materials?

The metal roof at the entrance will be zinc, the normal zinc that is always used on the roofs in France. And the glass should end up about the same greenish quality as on the model. That hasn't been figured out really yet either. The best glass I've seen so far, even including the Pei Pyramid, is still the Grand Palais. The windows there are really great. I like them because of their handmade quality.

– No chain link in this building?

No chain link. I'm not really doing much with it right now. When I worked with it, I was dealing with what I had and the materials that were affordable. I'm optimistic. I think the little Danziger building that I did in Melrose in 1964 (in Los Angeles) still looks good. A 25-year-old building made with cheap materials and it looks as good as the library building downtown. I'm very careful about detailing materials to keep them intact; but in being careful I'm also careful about preserving the quality of immediacy.

– When you were talking earlier about the relationship between art and architecture, you used the term "moment of truth." Can you elaborate on your moments of truth?

The moment of truth is when you have to face yourself and put down the first line or the first brush stroke if you're an artist. There is a point where I have to make a decision, take a direction. There are a lot of them in a building. It's essentially what makes a building look like it does, like the American Center building, which is the aggregate of all those moments of truth and my selection. It's what the shape of a building will be, which comes from inside your own values, unless you copy other stuff.

– You have said that if your American Center building looks at all like a particular person, it looks like Henry Pillsbury. Can you explain that?

Well, the building is a direct result of my conversations with Henry. It is completely about my involvement with him, my understanding of his vision for the Center, what it's going to do in the future, what it will mean to people who use it. It came out of our dialogue and hours and hours of conversation. He has worked closely on every aspect of it.

– So this building has been a collaborative effort?

Collaboration is a necessity for me. It's necessary in general in my work. Absolutely essential. Cities are built by a lot of people.

– It's tempting to draw comparisons between this building and the building that Peter Eisenman has just finished for the Wexner Center for the Visual Arts on the campus of The Ohio State University in Columbus, Ohio]. Since you and Peter Eisenman are both known as deconstructivist architects. . .

I am not a deconstructivist! That term really drives me crazy. It's like someone invented this word and took my work, which I've been doing for more than twenty years, long before the word was invented, and crammed me into it. People insist on putting us in a box. They can't be comfortable with something they can't categorize. It's true that I'm very interested in buildings that are open, that allow people in them. But my buildings have always been that way because I'm interested in openness and accessibility, not just in structural devices.

– Well, the Wexner Center building is very idiosyncratic. It is a very personal statement by its architect, Peter Eisenman, and there is a great deal of curiosity about how that building will work with art in it, and whether or not the design will compete with the Wexner Center's program over the long haul. How difficult is it to make a personal architectural statement when you are designing a building for arts programming?

The American Center building won't compete with program. It's about program. It's completely a response to the client. I'll tell you a story: At a certain point after I'd talked to Henry and Judith [Judith Pisar, Chairman of the Board of the American Center in Paris], I saw all of the problems because they have this specific budget and this limited amount of real estate and they want a place to handle all of the programming they are talking about. A lot of programming, very complex. And as the architect, I am supposed to take all of their problems and give them back a thing, a building, a place that works for their program. That is when I went back to Los Angeles to my office and had eight weeks of panic. And Henry and Judith kept calling and saying, "What's happening?" They wanted to watch me work. They wanted to see solutions. They wanted to take Polaroid pictures of models and see drawings. And I wouldn't take their calls. I told them to leave me alone and go away, to let me work it out. I had to find the answers for myself, my moments of truth. I had to deal with the problems and figure them out my own way. So, ultimately, this building is just as much my personal statement as Peter Eisenman's is his in Columbus. Mine is based on the information and the problems I was given by my client and this building is a direct answer, a personal answer to those problems.

– *How much of a problem is the development of Bercy for you? How do you deal with a site where, eventually, thirteen other projects will surround you? Do you try to stand out? How do you make an original statement and still not be overpowering or out of scale?*

It's a judgment call of where you pull in the reins and where you express yourself. Mostly that's done poorly by people. Most buildings that are built don't pay any attention to that. I think most good architects are sensitive to those issues and deal with them in some way or other. People hire an architect for his expression, for his talent to put things together in a certain way. I look at a situation such as Bercy optimistically. My perception has always been to deal with the world the way it is and to deal with it optimistically. I don't try to change it because I know I can't, so I try to fit in and mess with at the same time. Working in the city requires more than a passive interaction.

– *And how about technical problems? What place do they have in the artistry of architecture?*

Solving all the functional problems is an intellectual exercise. That is a different part of my brain. It's not less important, it's just different. And I make a value out of solving all those problems. Dealing with the context and the client and finding my moment of truth after I understand the problem. If you look at our process, the firm's process, you see models that show the pragmatic solution to the building without architecture. Then you see the study models that go through leading to the final scheme. We start with shapes, sculptural forms. Then we work into the technical stuff.

– *How do you feel about the legacy of your buildings?*

I'm not that precious about myself. On the other hand, these are public buildings that have to maintained. There's a responsibility. The community invests money and there is a necessity that the building exists for a number of years and be built out of substantial materials.

– *It seems as though many architects have been trying to make their buildings seem more important, more substantial, by appropriating a lot of forms and details from the past, by turning to Neo Classicism.*

You know, I got very angry when other architects started making buildings that look like Greek temples. I thought it was a denial of the present. It's a rotten thing to do to our children. It's as if we're telling them there's nothing to do but look back. It's like there's no reason to be optimistic about the future. So I got angry. That's really when I started drawing the fish, because the fish has been around for thousands and thousands of years. It's a natural creature, very fluid. It's a continuous form and it survives. And it's not contrived. To tell you the truth, I didn't intend for it to become a central form when it first occurred to me. It was an instinctive thing.

– *Will there be any fish at the new American Center?*

So far, there is no fish form in the building at all. If one were to come, it might happen in the accueil. The plaza around the building has a pattern of paving that is like fish scales. So I guess that's the fish surfacing.

– *The fish is a very appealing symbol particularly in these confused times when the whole world seems to be in a state of upheaval and change. Pluralism seems to dominate architecture today. Does this make for incoherence, or do you think it just reflects the incoherence of the world today?*

This is a time of incoherence, chaos, rushing around. It is a time of serious global problems that we can't solve and don't even understand most of the time. As far as architecture is concerned, I think pluralism reflects the times in America. It may not be a positive thing in Europe; I can't make that judgement. But certainly in America we have been hit by waves and waves of European architects in our teaching institutions to the point where kids in architecture school feel like they're second-class citizens in their own country. This was true when I went to Harvard and it is the same now. There has been an inferiority complex over the years. You have to hope that original people will get over that.

– *How much freedom does an architect have in his work?*

There is not a lot that good architects get to do because basically the value systems are mostly about what architects are hired to do. Those are the priorities in America. This is a country that spends less per capita on culture than most smaller European countries. So we're still in the woods a bit on that one. I think it's been wonderful that the American press has started to focus on American architecture. There has been enough stuff made so there is a dialogue. There has been an awakening of architects. You certainly see it in Los Angeles. I think pluralism is wonderful. That is the American way. Individual expression. It hasn't hurt us in painting and sculpture. It hasn't hurt us in literature and it won't hurt us in architecture.

PETER PRAN & CARLOS ZAPATA

ELLERBE BECKET

Canadian National Trust Development

J F KENNEDY AIRPORT NEW YORK

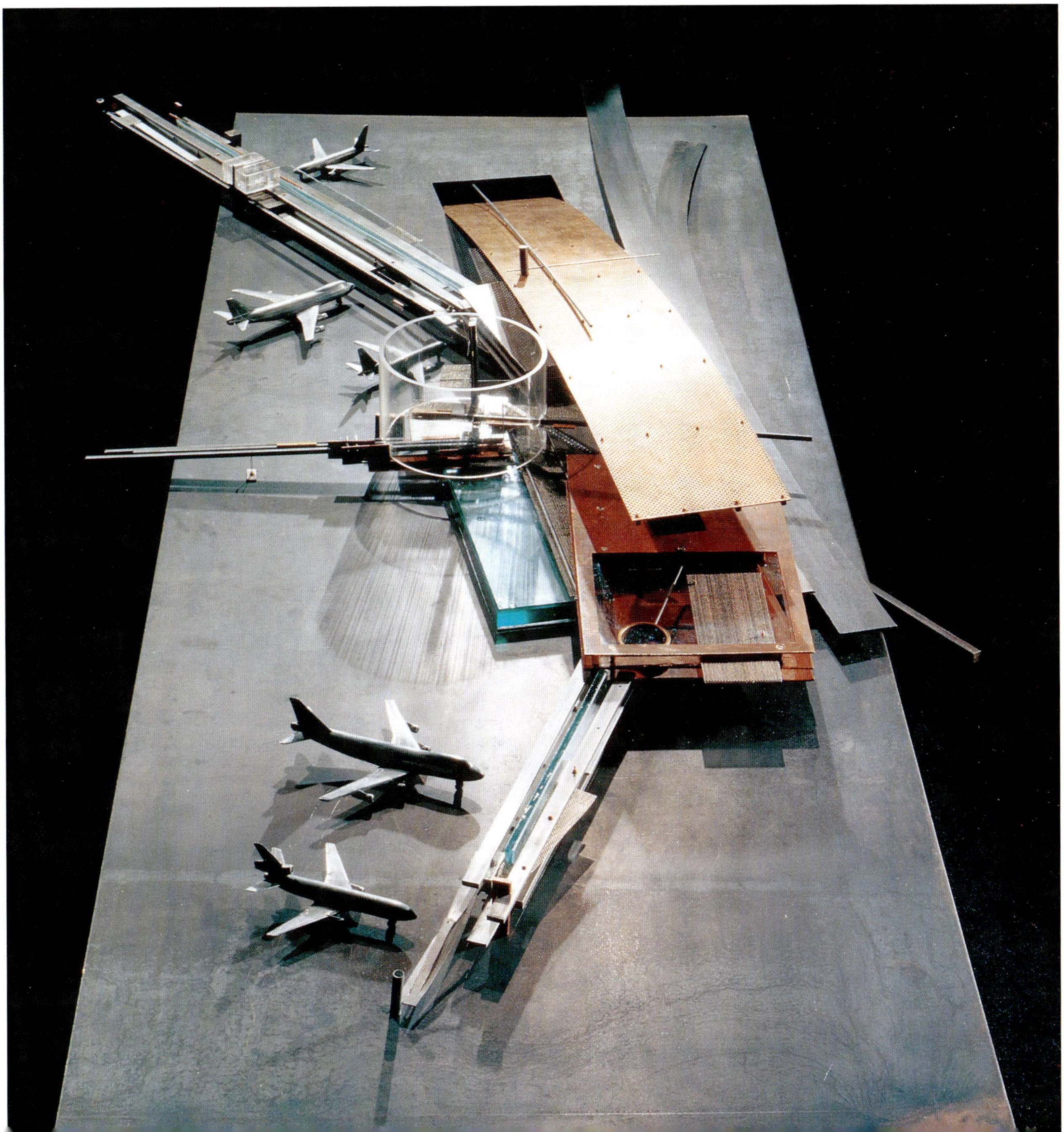

UNIVERSITY OF MINNESOTA SCHOOL OF ARCHITECTURE

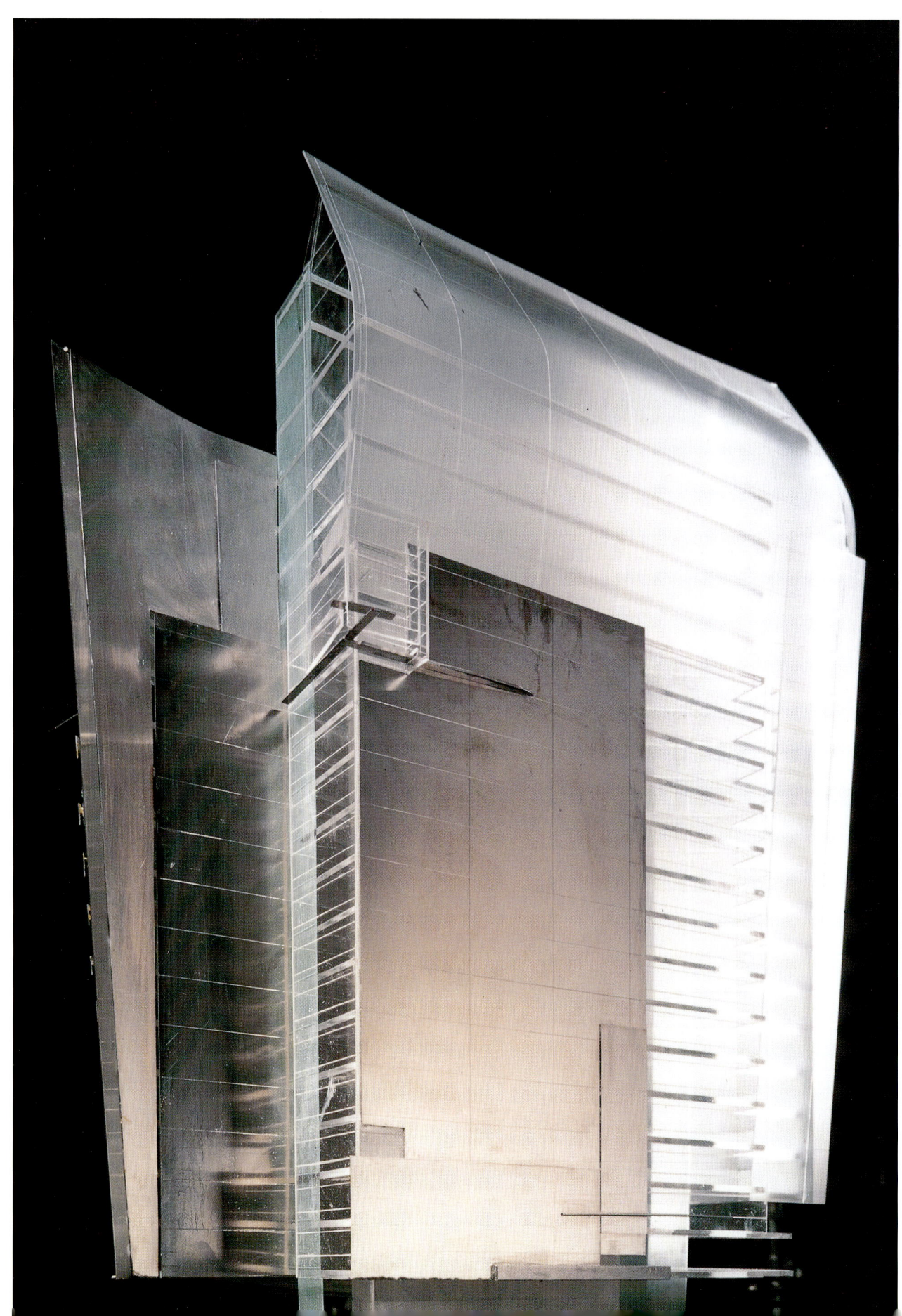

BANCO POPULAR ECUADOR

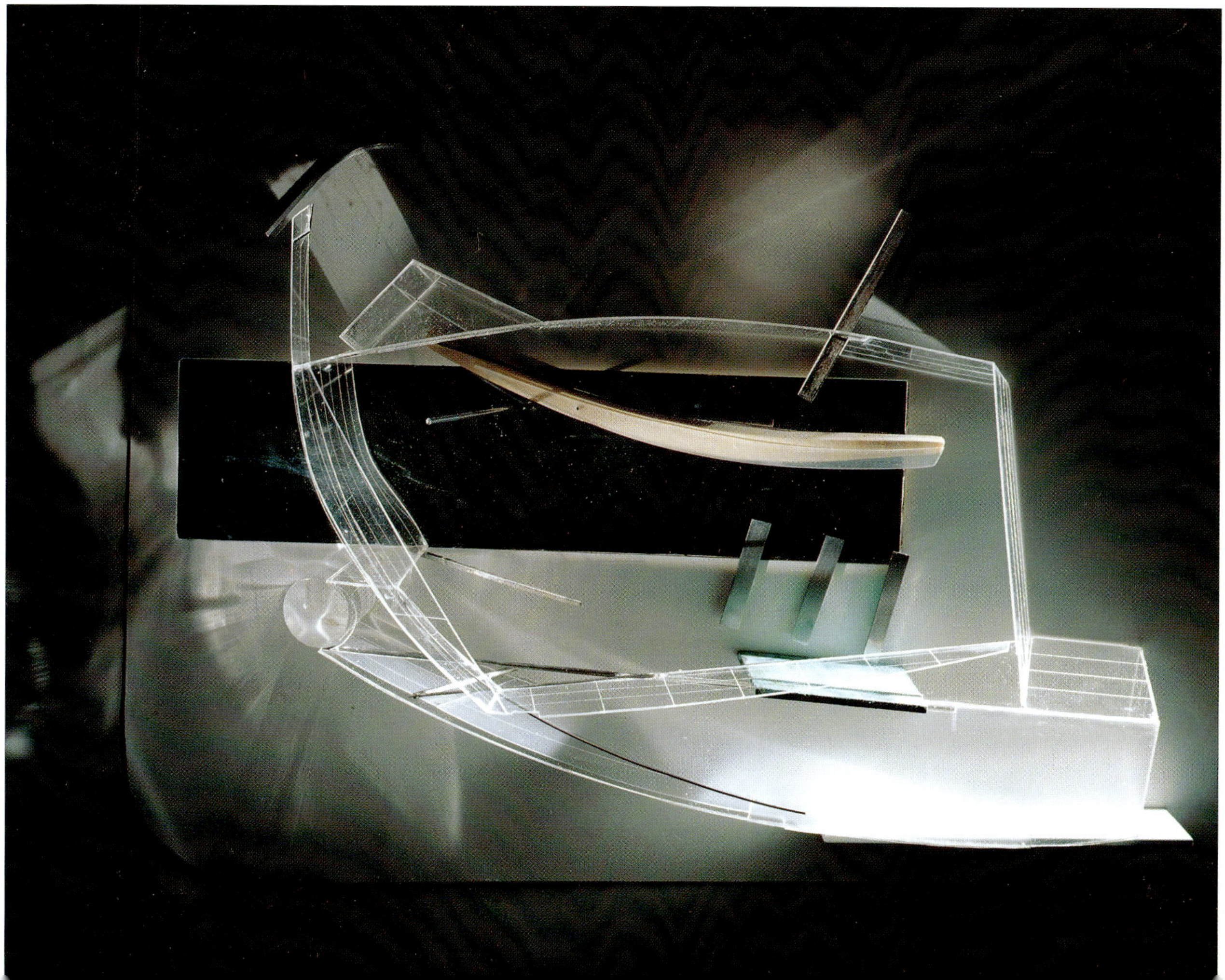

BOLLES-WILSON
URBANISTIC UNIT KRAKOW

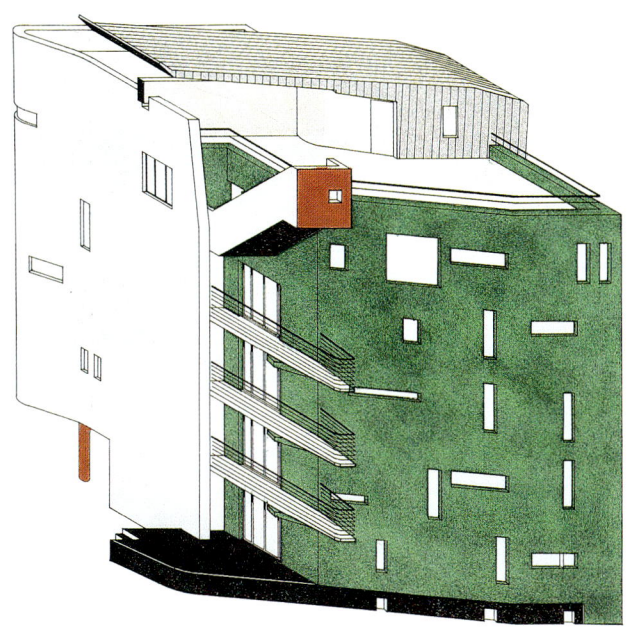

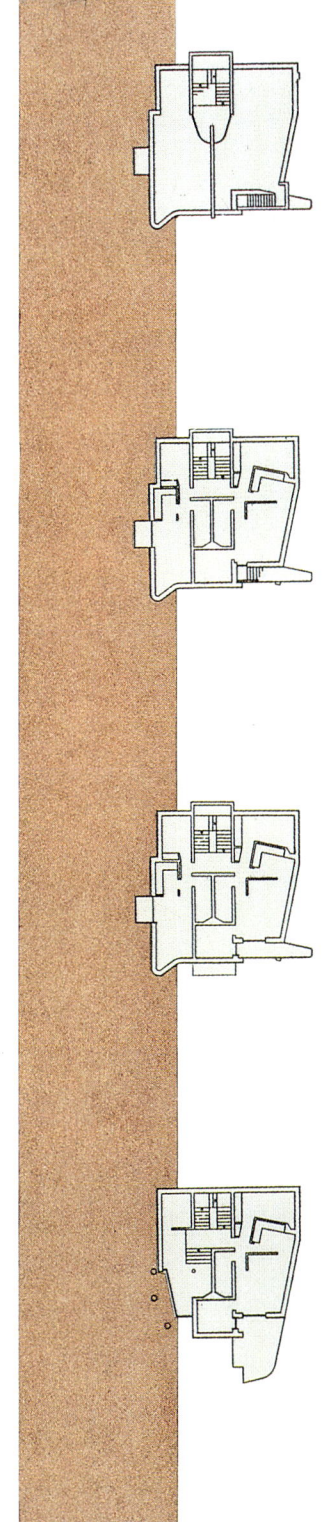

There are places where architecture is in closest pursuit of actual contemporary issues (Japan, Spain). There are also always those other places which at a particular time receive more than they dispense, places where habit obscures vision (England, Poland). To be invited to design an Urban villa (social housing unit) in Krakow is an opportunity to explore connections between what is referred to in Poland as new constructivism and a modernist tradition interrupted by social realism, quantitative system building and post modernism. Eight apartment houses have been designed by invited polish and foreign architects for the Debniki Urban Complex, an experimental program coordinated by Atelier Loegler and Partners.

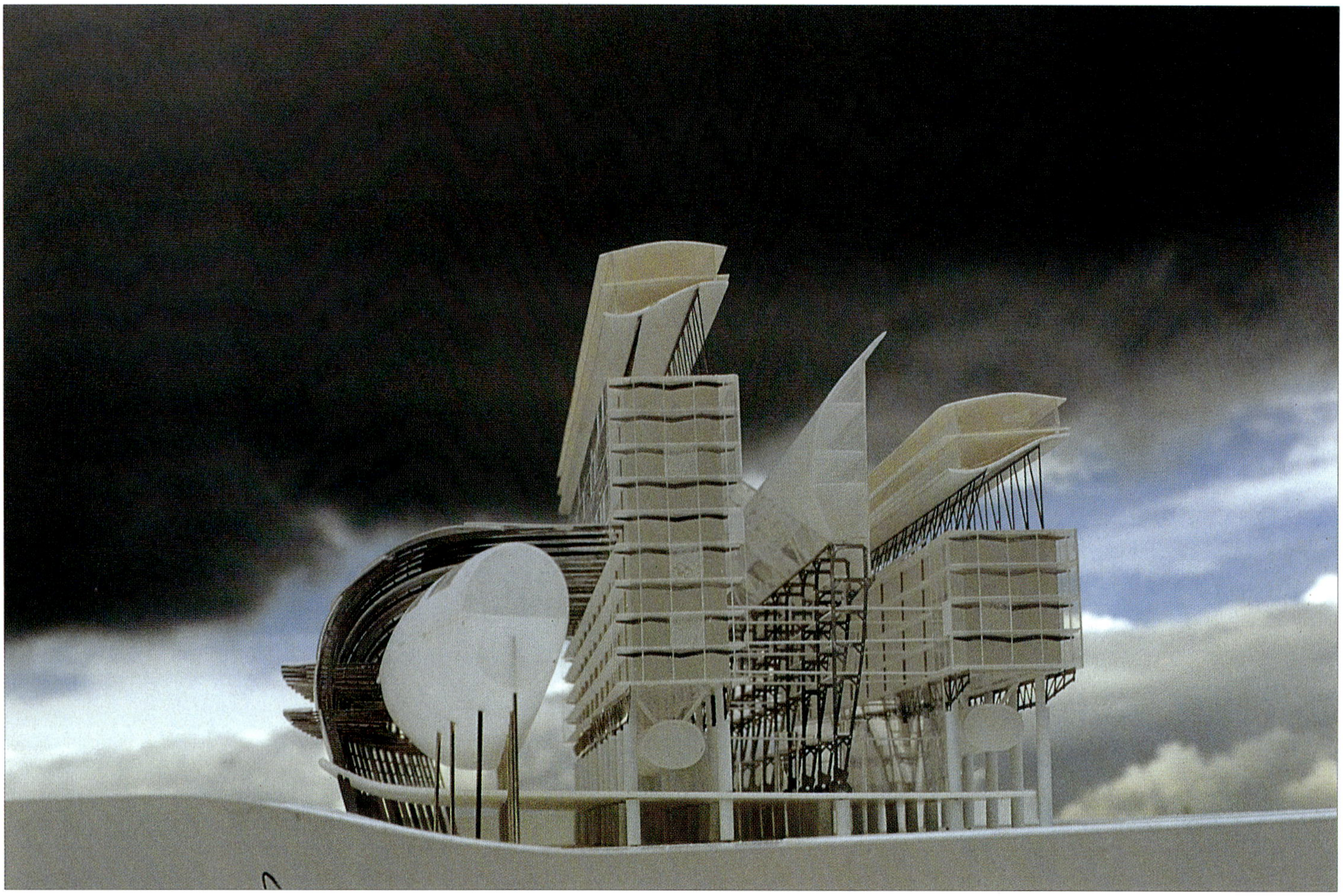

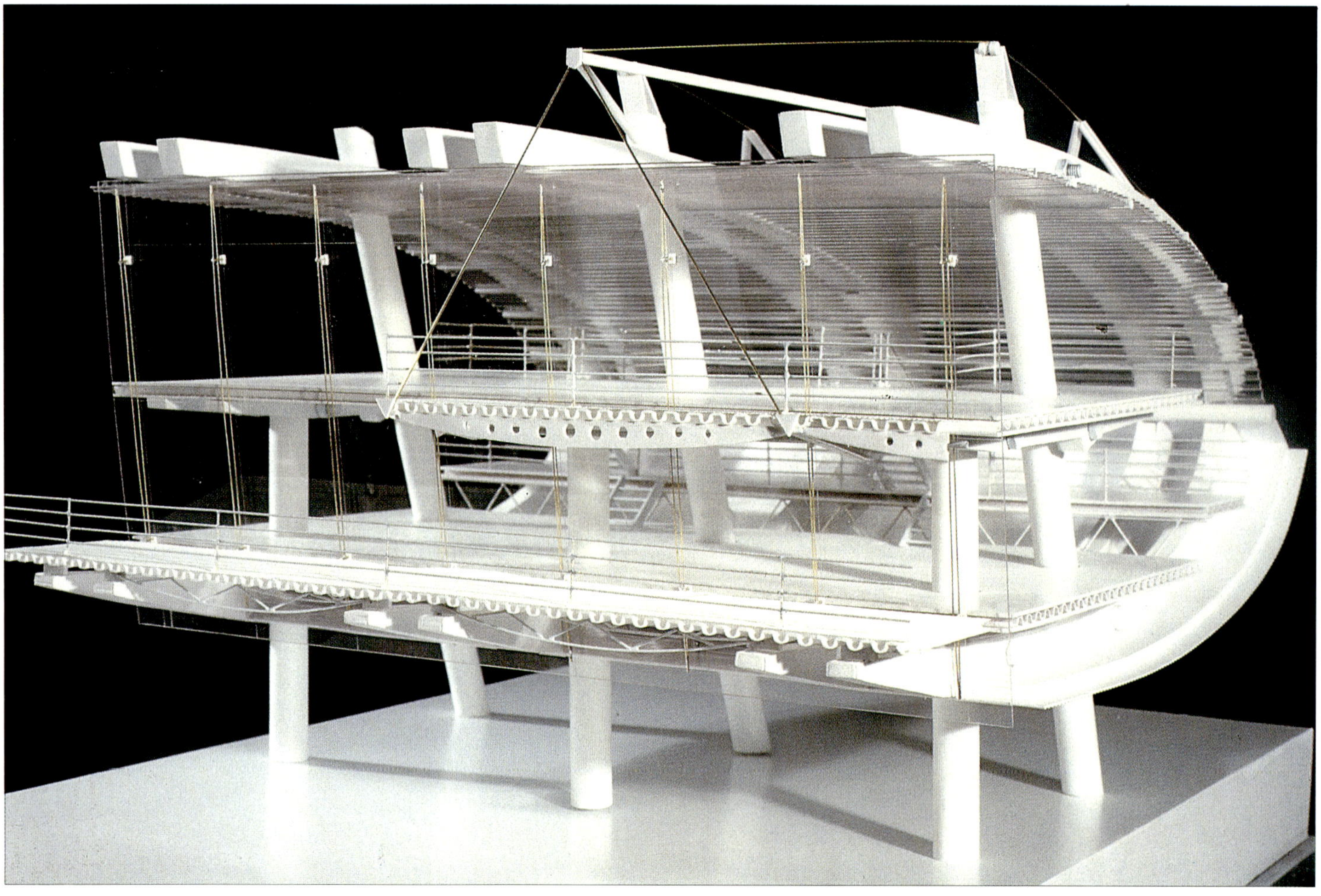

La Cathédrale Engloutie

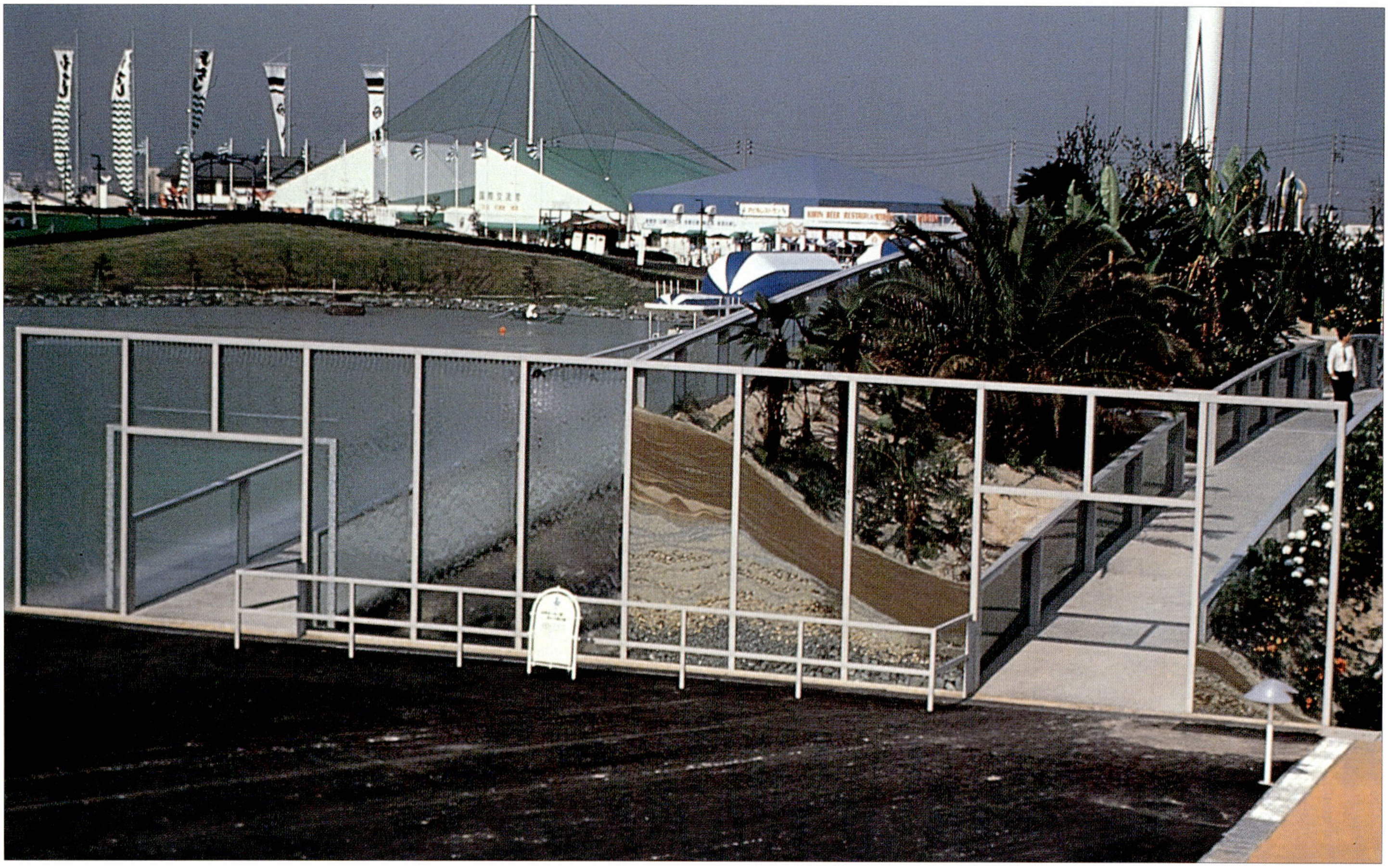

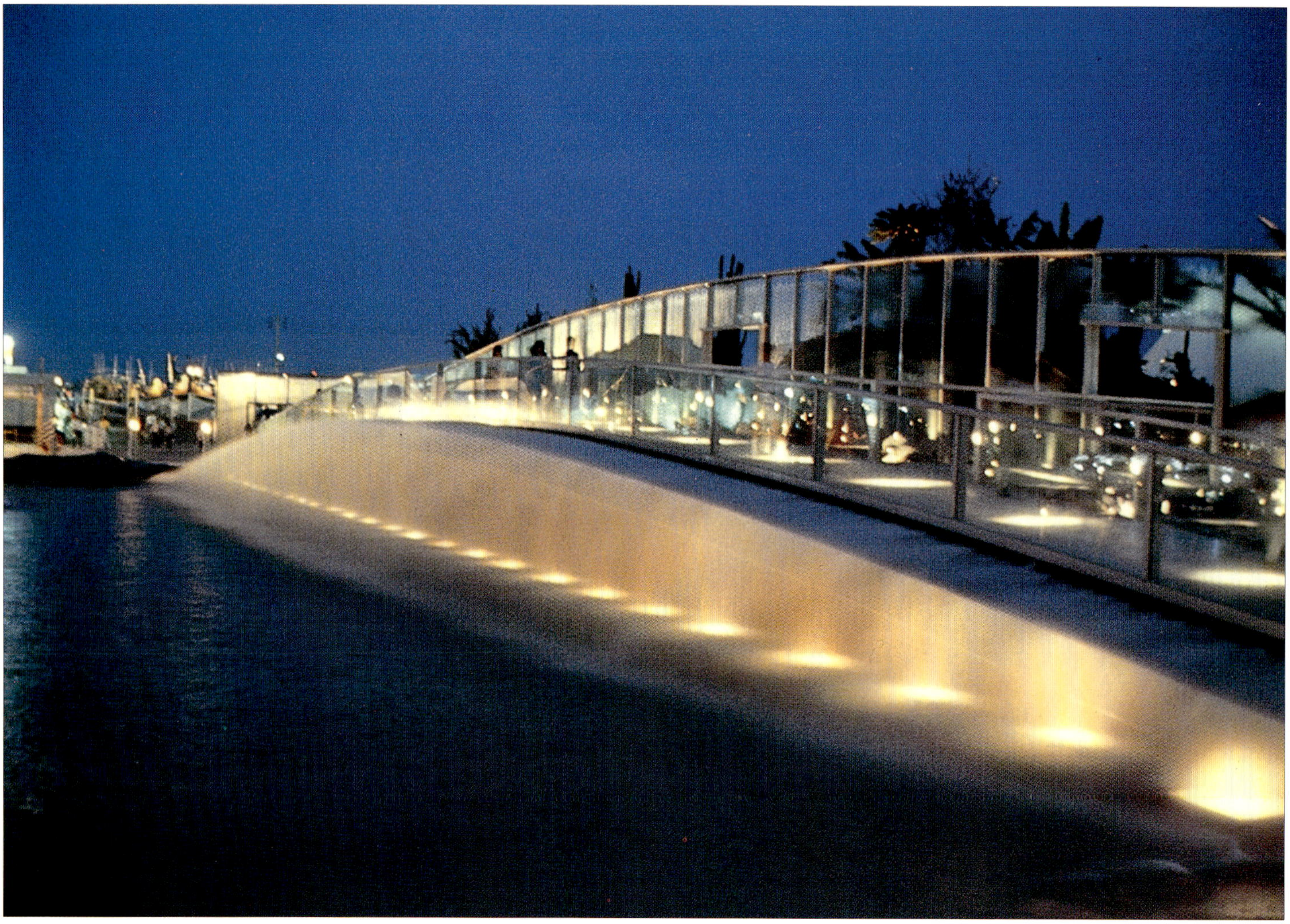

SITE

FOUR CONTINENTS BRIDGE JAPAN

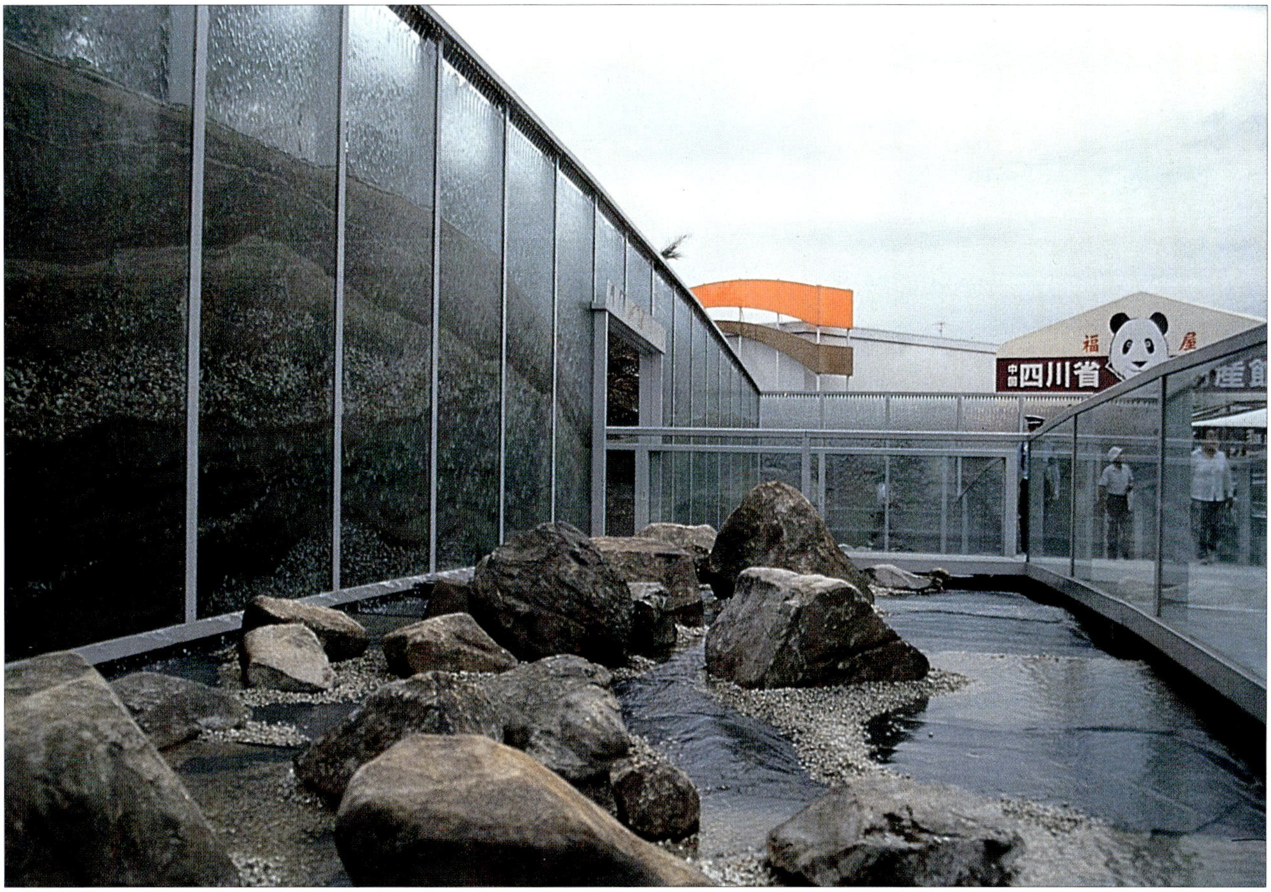

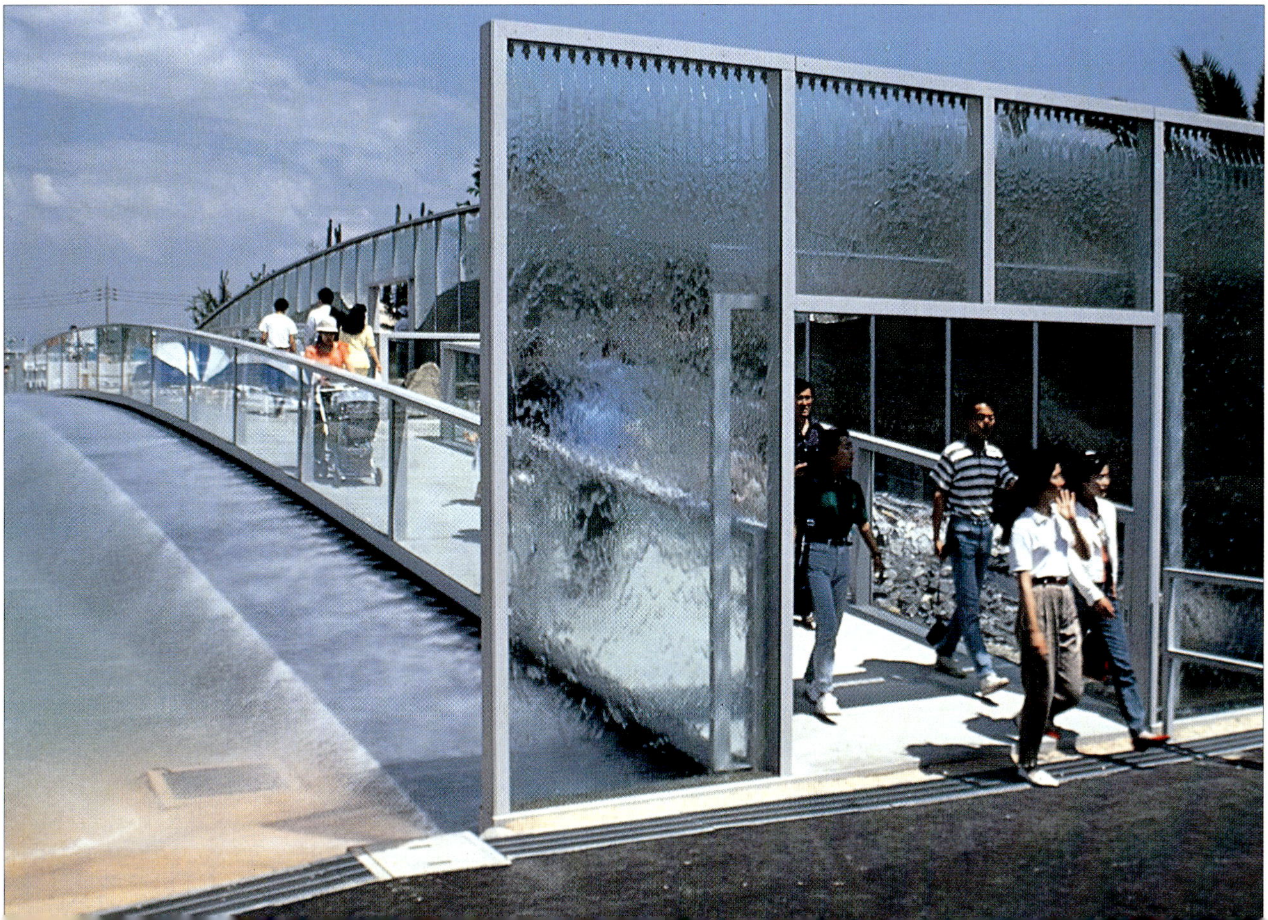

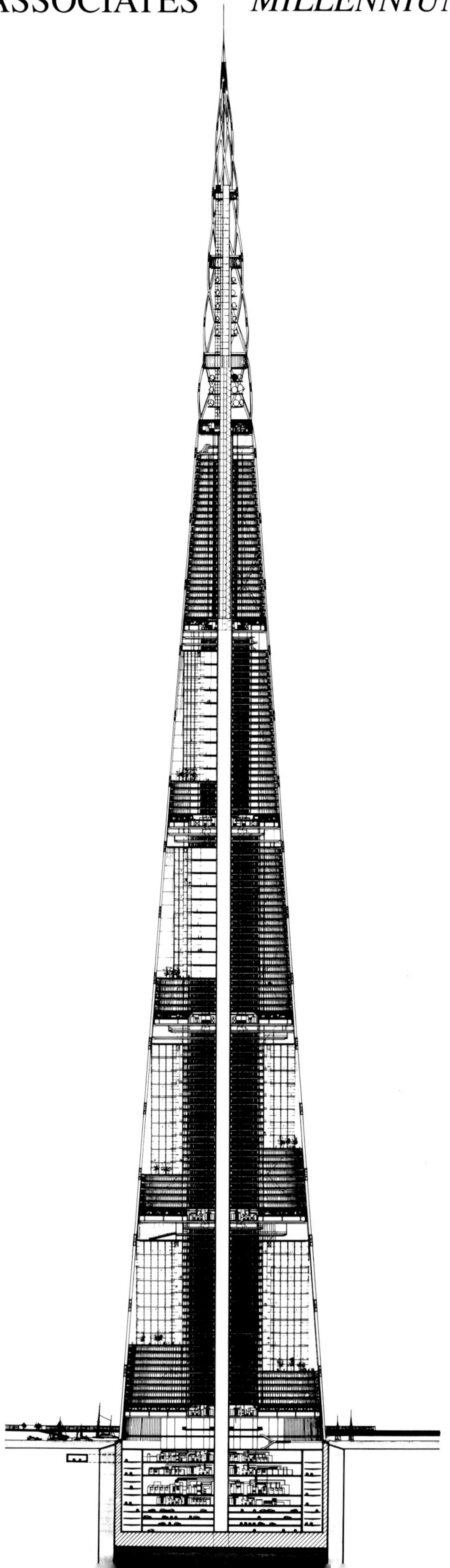

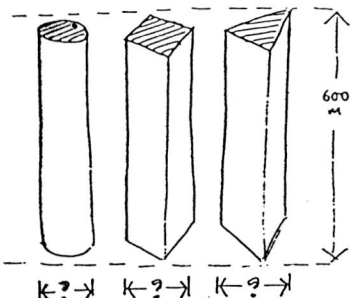

① OUR STARTING POINT IS TO LOOK AT 3 BASIC GEOMETRIC FORMS. AND CONSIDER THEM PRIMARILY FROM A WIND LOADING STAND POINT AS WE UNDERSTAND THIS TO BE THE PRIME GENERATOR FOR TALL BUILDING DESIGN. (SEISMIC LOADING CAUSES LESS CONSTRAINTS.)

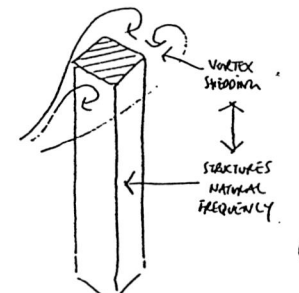

VORTEX SHEDDING

STRUCTURES NATURAL FREQUENCY

② WE ALSO UNDERSTAND THAT THERE IS A DIRECT RELATIONSHIP BETWEEN THE STRUCTURES OWN NATURAL FREQUENCY AND THE WAY THE VORTEX IS SHED BY THE SHAPE OF THE BUILDING

③ WE ∴ NEED TO KNOW MORE ABOUT HOW THE VARIOUS SHAPES EFFECT AIR MOVEMENTS.

 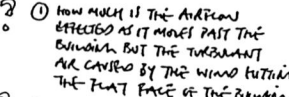

❓① HOW MUCH IS THE AIRFLOW EFFECTED AS IT MOVES PAST THE BUILDING BUT THE TURBULENT AIR CAUSED BY THE WIND HITTING THE FLAT FACE OF THE BUILDING?

❓② HOW LONG DOES THE VORTEX TAKE TO DISSIPATE AND DOES ITS INFLUENCE DIMINISH OR INCREASE?

❓③ HOW IS THE AIRFLOW PAST THE BUILDING EFFECTED BY THE VORTEX? WHAT HAPPENS?

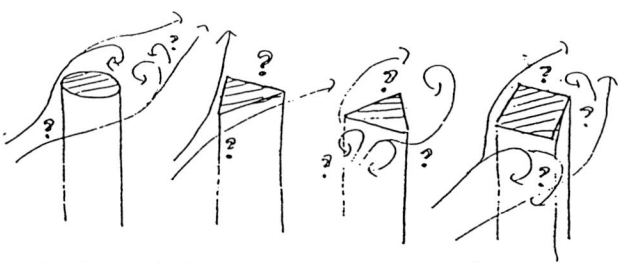

WHAT HAPPENS AS THE WIND HITS VARIOUS SHAPES? IS ANY OVERALL SHAPE BETTER THAN THE OTHERS? BY STUDY CAN WE GENERATE ENOUGH INFORMATION TO HELP US EXTEND THE FORM OF THE BUILDING → WIND TUNNEL TESTS?

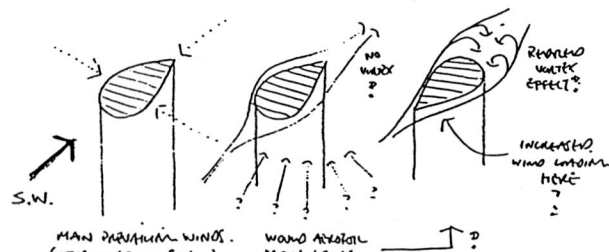

S.W.

MAIN PREVAILING WINDS (+ TYPHOONS FROM S.W.)

NO VORTEX?

REVERSED VORTEX EFFECT?

WOULD AEROFOIL PROFILE HELP?

INCREASED WIND LOADING HERE?

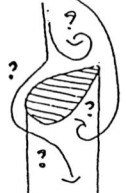 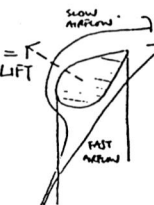

= LIFT

SLOW AIRFLOW

FAST AIRFLOW

WITH SUCH A DIRECTIONAL SHAPE WOULD THE EFFECTS OF WIND FROM DIFFERENT DIRECTIONS GENERATE MORE COMPLEX AND ∴ LESS CONTROLLABLE SIDE EFFECTS?

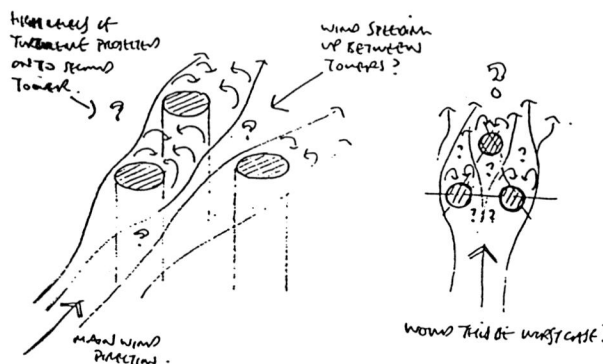

HIGH LEVELS OF TURBULENCE PROJECTED ON TO SECOND TOWER?

WIND SPEEDING UP BETWEEN TOWERS?

MAIN WIND DIRECTION

WOULD THIRD BE WORST CASE?

BUT:- IF THE "OPENING" EFFECT OF SUCH A COMPOSITE TOWER REDUCES LOADING TO AN ACCEPTABLE LIMIT......

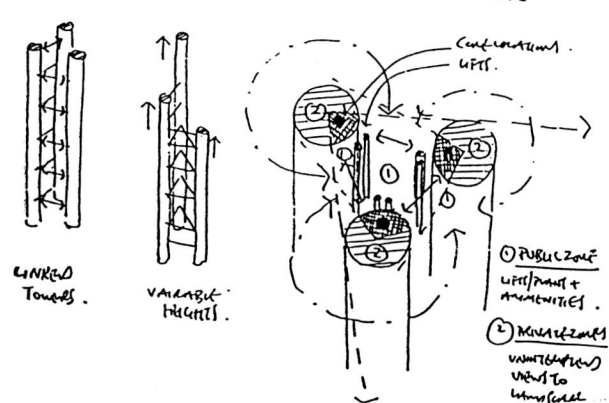

LINKED TOWERS.

VARIABLE HEIGHTS.

CONFIGURATIONS. LIFTS.

① PUBLIC ZONE LIFT/PLANT + AMENITIES

② PRIVATE ZONES UNINTERRUPTED VIEWS TO LANDSCAPE

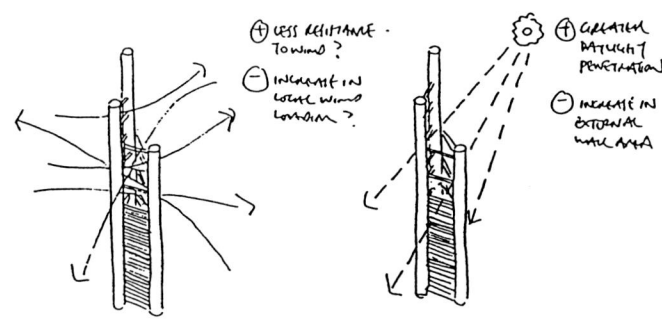

⊕ LESS RESISTANCE TO WIND?
⊖ INCREASE IN TOTAL WIND LOADING?

⊕ GREATER DAYLIGHT PENETRATION
⊖ INCREASE IN EXTERNAL WALL AREA

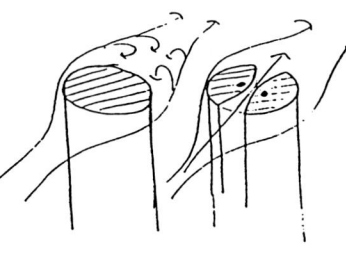

WITH CIRCULAR ELEMENT AIRFLOW PASSES AROUND CREATING A VORTEX:-
① COULD AIR BE DRAWN THROUGH SUCH A SHAPE TO SMOOTH OUT AIRFLOW?
② ALSO IF AIR DRAWN THROUGH A VENTURI COULD IT BE USED TO CREATE WIND ENERGY?

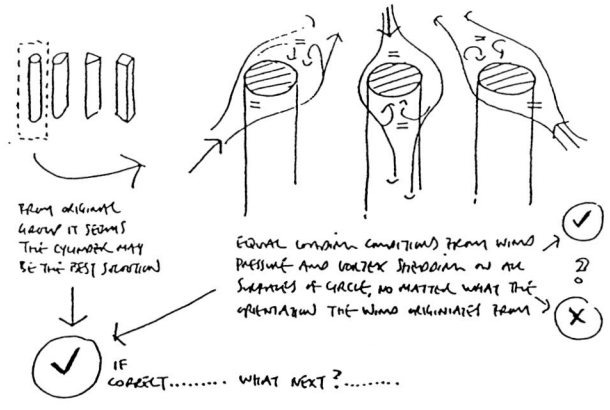

FROM ORIGINAL
GROW IT SEEMS
THE CYLINDER MAY
BE THE BEST SOLUTION

EQUAL LOADING CONDITIONS FROM WIND
PRESSURE AND VORTEX SHEDDING ON ALL
SURFACES OF CIRCLE, NO MATTER WHAT THE
ORIENTATION THE WIND ORIGINATES FROM

✓

IF
CORRECT......... WHAT NEXT?.........

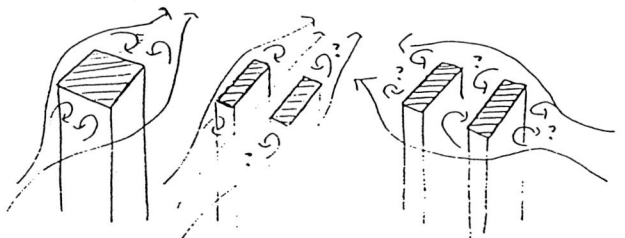

WITH ALL SOLID SHAPES THE WIND IS RESISTED BY THE BUILDING
AT A COMPLETE SEALED OBJECT. WHAT HAPPENS IF A MORE OPEN
FORM IS CONSIDERED? WOULD VORTEX SHEDDING BE
REDUCED? WOULD UNACCEPTABLE LOCAL LOADINGS BE GENERATED?

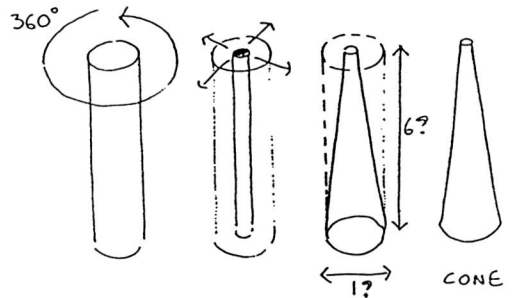

CONE

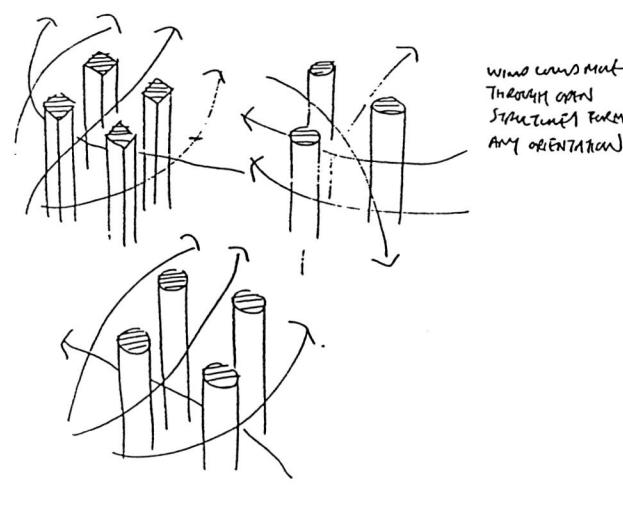

WIND LOADS MUST
THROUGH OPEN
STRUCTURES FORM
ANY ORIENTATION

WITH 'BLUEWATER' SITE THE VIEWS OUT FROM THE
BUILDING WILL BE 360°. THIS LEADS TO THE LOGIC
OF UTILIZING A CENTRAL CONE FOR MOMENT STABILITY
ETC. FREEING UP THE EXTERNAL FASCADE. REDUCING THE
BUILDING DOWN TOWARDS THE TOP HELPS LOADING &
STABILITY CREATING A 6-1 RATIO CYLINDRICAL CONE.

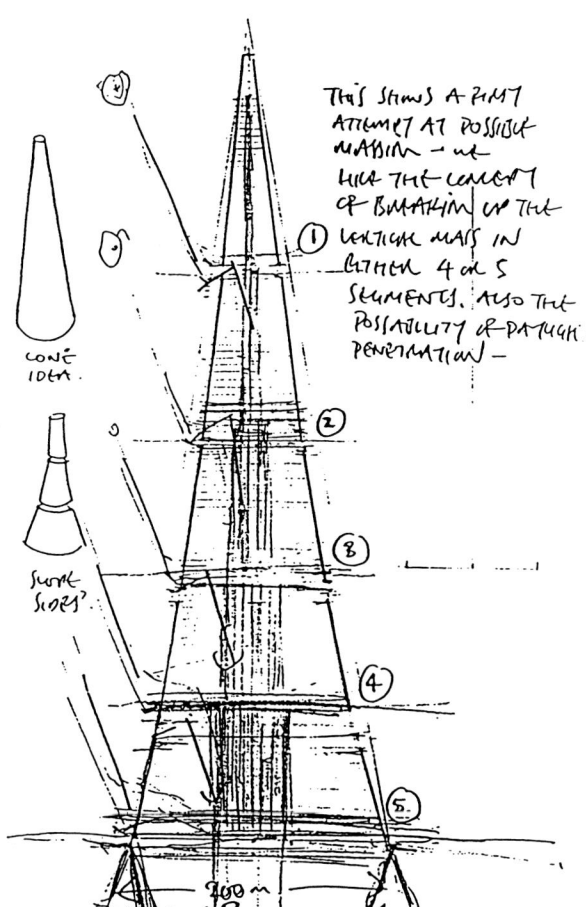

CONE
IDEA.

SLOPE
SIDES?

THIS SHOWS A FIRST
ATTEMPT AT POSSIBLE
MASSING – WE
LIKE THE CONCEPT
OF BREAKING UP THE
VERTICAL MASS IN
EITHER 4 OR 5
SEGMENTS. ALSO THE
POSSIBILITY OF DAYLIGHT
PENETRATION –

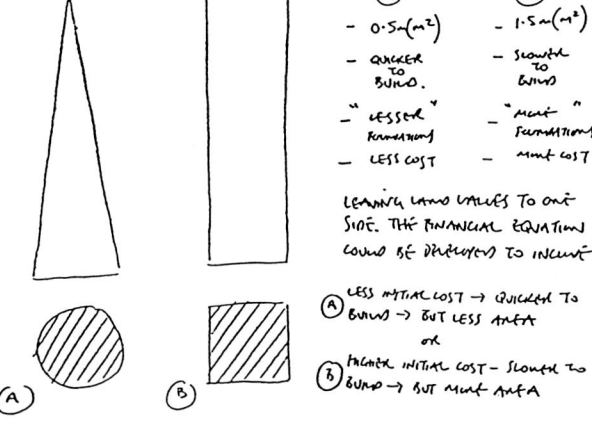

	(A)	(B)
	0·5m(m²)	1·5m(m²)
	QUICKER TO BUILD.	SLOWER TO BUILD
	'LESSER' FOUNDATIONS	'MORE' FOUNDATIONS
	LESS COST	MORE COST

LEANING LAND VALUES TO ONE
SIDE. THE FINANCIAL EQUATION
COULD BE DEVELOPED TO INCLUDE:

(A) LESS INITIAL COST → QUICKER TO
BUILD → BUT LESS AREA
OR
(B) HIGHER INITIAL COST → SLOWER TO
BUILD → BUT MORE AREA

TO US IT SUGGESTS THAT (A) MIGHT BE THE BETTER DIRECTION
IN OVERALL TERMS: BUT WHAT WE DO NOT KNOW IS HOW MUCH
SUCH A VENTURE OF BUILDING IS DEPENDENT ON THE AVAILABLE
SPACE AT THE END OF THE CONSTRUCTION. TO REALISE THE PROJECT
EARLIER AND THEREFORE MINIMIZING THE BUILDING PAYBACK TIME
SEEMS ATTRACTIVE HOWEVER.

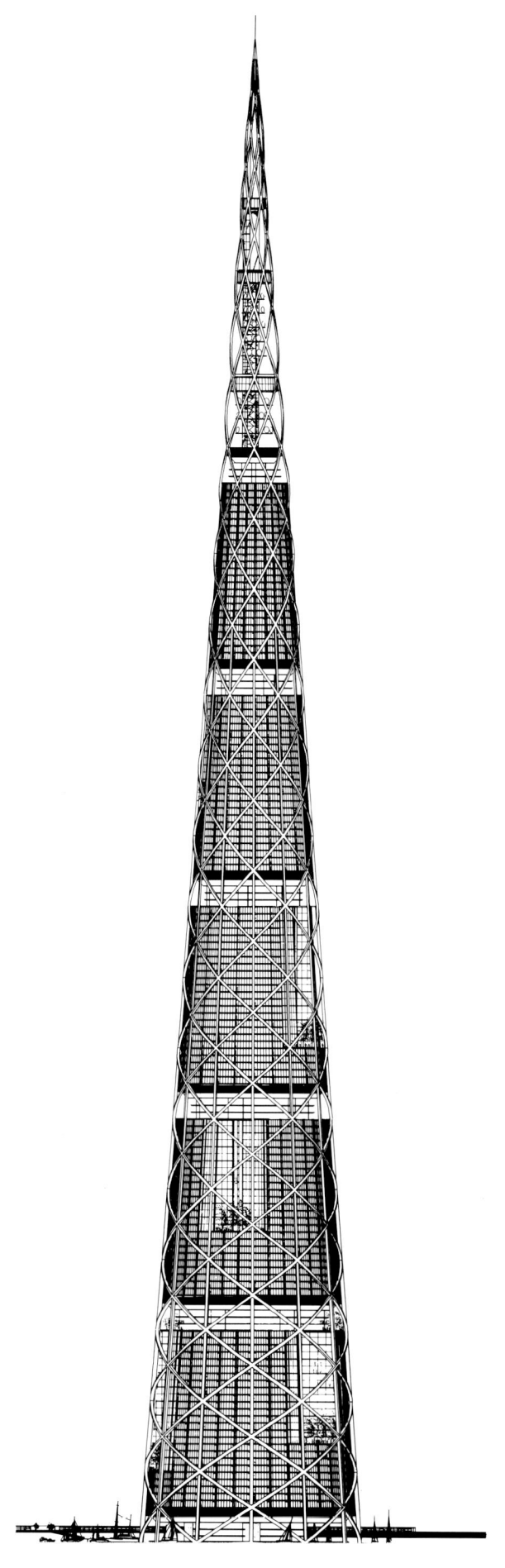

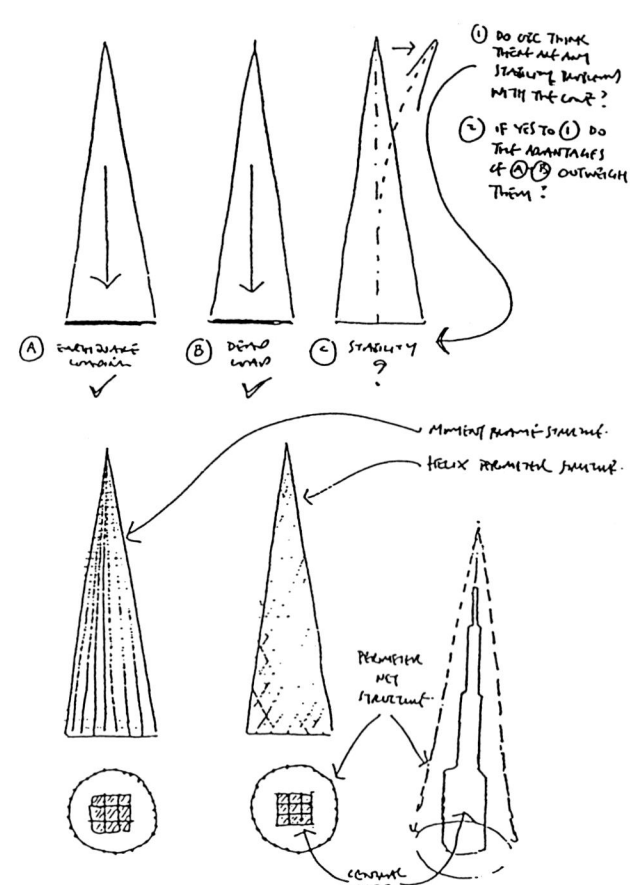

(A) ENGINEERED CONDITION ✓ (B) DEAD LOADS ✓ (C) STABILITY ?

① DO OBC THINK THERE ARE ANY STABILITY PROBLEMS WITH THE CONE?

② IF YES TO ① DO THE ADVANTAGES OF Ⓐ Ⓑ OUTWEIGH THEM?

MOMENT FRAME STRUCTURE
HELIX PERIMETER STRUCTURE
PERIMETER NET STRUCTURE
CENTRAL CORE

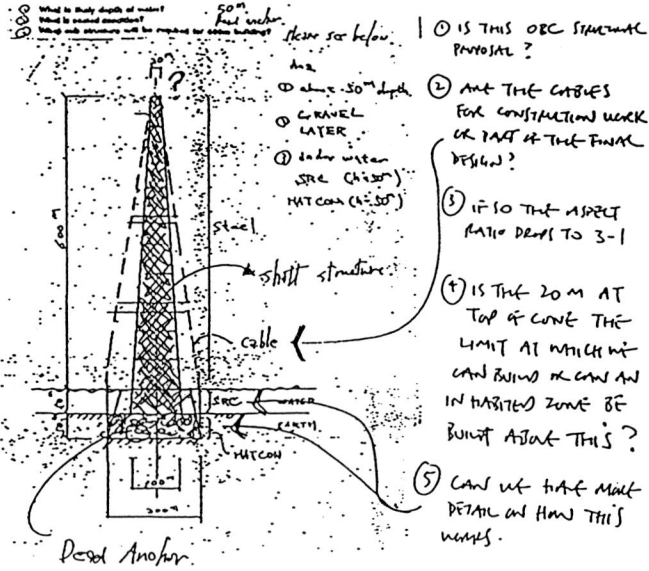

Detail Anchor.

① IS THIS OBC STRUCTURAL PROPOSAL?

② ARE THE CABLES FOR CONSTRUCTION WORK OR PART OF THE FINAL DESIGN?

③ IF SO THE ASPECT RATIO DROPS TO 3-1

④ IS THE 20 M AT TOP OF CONE THE LIMIT AT WHICH WE CAN BUILD OR CAN AN INHABITED ZONE BE BUILT ABOVE THIS?

⑤ CAN WE HAVE MORE DETAIL ON HOW THIS WORKS.

HOW CRITICAL IS THE SHEAR FLOW FOR A TRUNCATED CONE? DOES THIS GENERATE THE CABLES INDICATED ON THE ABOVE DIAGRAM? — IF SO CAN THE CORE + PERIMETER STRUCTURE OF THE CONE ALONE RESIST THIS AT A 6-1 OR 5-1 RATIO ???

MECHANICAL + ELECTRICAL PLANT.

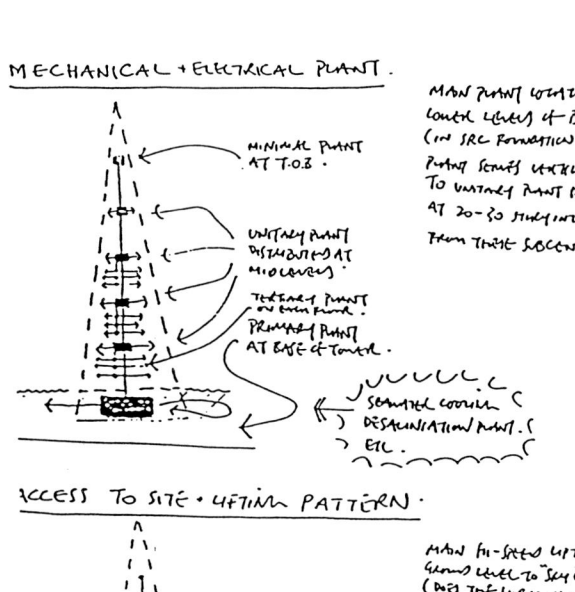

MINIMAL PLANT AT T.O.B.
UNITARY PLANT DISTRIBUTED AT MID LEVELS.
TERTIARY PLANT ON EACH FLOOR.
PRIMARY PLANT AT BASE OF TOWER.
SEAWATER COOLING
DESALINATION PLANT.
ETC.

MAIN PLANT LOCATED IN LOWER LEVELS OF BUILDING (IN SRC FORMATION CORE). PLANT SERVES VERTICALLY TO UNITARY PLANT DISTRIBUTED AT 20-30 STOREY INTERVALS. FROM THESE SUB CENTRES

ALTERNATIVE ENERGY.

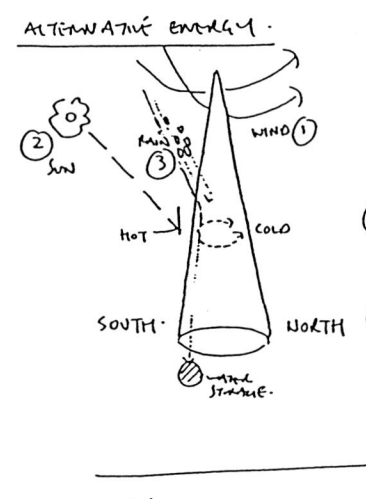

WIND ①
SUN ②
③
HOT   COLD
SOUTH   NORTH

① IF WIND SPEED NOT USABLE ON A LARGE SCALE WOULD THERE BE ANY BENEFIT IN USING IT AT TOP OF BUILDING IN SOME SMALL FORM? WE ARE ASSUMING ANSWER IS NO.

② CAN WE EXPLOIT THE NORTH/SOUTH ORIENTATIONS IN TERMS OF SOLAR CONDITION ON SOUTH + HEAT PUMPS ETC TO NORTH + VISE VERSA??

③ SHOULD WE COLLECT RAINWATER + PROCESS FOR WATER USE IN BUILDING (DO WE RELY ON DESALINATION OR WATER PIPED IN?)

ACCESS TO SITE + LIFTING PATTERN

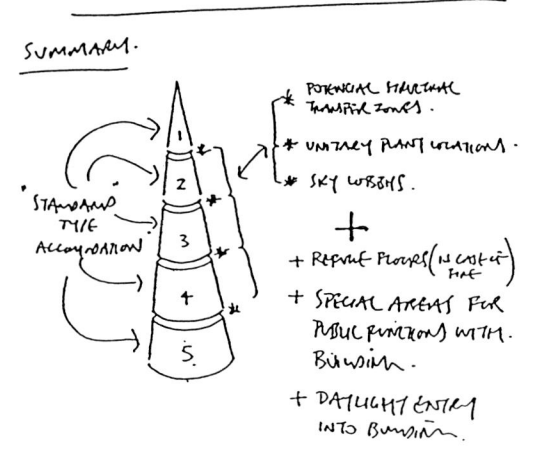

MAIN HI-SPEED LIFTING
STANDARD LIFTS FOR EACH ZONE.
ESCALATOR ACCESS THROUGH SPECIAL AREAS.
RAIL AND / OR ROAD BRIDGE?
SUBWAY?

MAIN HI-SPEED LIFTS FROM GROUND LEVEL TO "SKY LOBBIES" - (DOES THE LARGE MOTOR IDEA MAKE SENSE FOR A BUILDING OF 600m?) CONVENTIONAL LIFTING WITHIN EACH ZONE.

ESCALATOR ACCESS AT "SPECIAL" + PUBLIC AREAS WITHIN BUILDING

WHAT ABOUT PEOPLE ACCESS TO SITE?? — IS A ROAD BRIDGE FEASIBLE?

IS A SUBWAY LINK FEASIBLE?

BOTH?

SUMMARY.

POTENTIAL STRUCTURAL TRANSFER ZONES.
UNITARY PLANT LOCATIONS.
SKY LOBBIES.

STANDARD TYPE ACCOMMODATION

+ REFUGE FLOORS (IN CASE OF FIRE)

+ SPECIAL AREAS FOR PUBLIC FUNCTIONS WITHIN BUILDING.

+ DAYLIGHT ENTRY INTO BUILDING.

An Invitation to The Second Annual

International Architecture Book Fair

AIA Convention and Exposition, May 16-19, 1991, Washington, D.C.

The finest in architectural publishing was captured when over 70 publishers from around the world exhibited at The American Institute of Architects' first Annual International Architecture Book Fair. We invite you to attend the second International Architecture Book Fair in Washington, D.C.

Whether you're interested in buying architecture books, writing them, buying or selling rights, or reviewing them, you should come to the Fair. Bookstore and book club buyers; architects and other design professionals; librarians; students, deans, faculty; architecture reviewers, critics, authors; publishing and bookstore media; and AIA Chapter leaders are all invited to attend.

See and learn more at the Architecture Book Fair than you could in months of individual contacts with this most impressive assembly of international publishers. Find out about special Fair discounts, attend booksignings, win books, discover new titles, present your manuscript, and learn about trends in architectual publishing.

"The Architecture Book Fair was wonderful! Not only were the librarians anxious to attend, the architects were just as excited!"

—Laura Dickinson, Chair,
   Association of Architectural Librarians

"I really appreciated the presence of so many foreign architectural publishers; the Fair had a truly international flavor."

—Susan Ford,
   Ballenford Architectural Books

"In reflecting on the convention and its highlights, the major item that still stands out is the Book Fair ...this was a veritable beehive of interest."

—Eugene J. Mackey III, AIA,
   Principal, Mackey Associates, P.C.

Over 70 publishers of books, journals, and posters participated in 1990, including 25 from 11 foreign countries.

*For more information or to reserve a free Book Fair pass
please contact:*

**The American Institute of Architects
International Architecture Book Fair
1735 New York Avenue, NW, Washington, DC 20006, USA
Phone: (202) 626-7395 • FAX: (202) 626-7518**

ARCHITECTURAL DESIGN

1990 ANNUAL SUBSCRIPTION RATE (for six double issues inc p&p) *Architectural Design*, UK only £49.50. Europe £59.50. Overseas US$99.50. Reduced Student Rate: UK £45. Europe £55. Overseas US$89.50. Subscriptions may be back-dated to any issue.

... 1 ARATA ISOZAKI
    0 85670 330 3   £3.95

... 3 TAFURI/CULOT/KRIER
    0 85670 355 9   £3.95

... 4 POST-MODERNISM
    0 85670 356 7   £3.95

... 11 SURREALISM
    0 85670 409 1   £6.95

... 14 HAND-BUILT HORNBY
    0 85670 430 X   £3.95

... 16 BRUCE GOFF
    0 85670 432 6   £6.95

... 19 SAINSBURY CENTRE
    0 85670 563 2   £3.95

... 20 ROMA INTERROTTA
    0 85670 560 8   £6.95

... 21 LEON BATTISTA ALBERTI
    0 85670 559 4   £6.95

... 22 HAWKSMOOR'S CHRISTCHURCH
    0 85670 650 7   £3.95

... 23 NEO-CLASSICISM
    0 85670 626 4   £6.95

... 24 BRITAIN IN THE 30s
    0 85670 627 2   £6.95

... 25 AALTO AND AFTER
    0 85670 701 5   £4.95

... 27 VIOLLET-LE-DUC
    0 85670 688 4   £6.95

... 31 URBANITY
    0 85670 746 5   £6.95

... 33 BRITISH ARCHITECTS 1981
    0 85670 750 3   £6.95

... 34 ROMANTIC HOUSES
    0 85670 754 6   £4.95

... 37 ANGLO AMERICAN SUBURB
    0 85670 690 6   £6.95

... 38 CURRENT PROJECTS
    0 85670 768 6   £4.95

... 44 FOREST EDGE & BERLIN
    0 85670 789 9   £8.95

... 46 DOLLS' HOUSES
    0 85670 827 5   £8.95

... 47 THE RUSSIAN AVANT-GARDE
    0 85670 832 1   £8.95

... 49 ELEMENTS OF ARCHITECTURE
    0 85670 834 8   £8.95

... 51 URBANISM
    0 85670 843 7   £8.95

... 53 BUILDING & RATIONAL ARCH
    0 85670 848 8   £8.95

... 54 LEON KRIER
    0 85670 844 5   £8.95

... 55 IAKOV CHERNIKHOV
    0 85670 841 0   £8.95

... 56 UIA CAIRO INT. EXHIBITION
    0 85670 852 6   £8.95

... 57 AMERICAN ARCHITECTURE
    0 85670 855 0   £8.95

... 58 REVISION OF THE MODERN
    0 85670 861 5   £8.95

... 59 SCHOOL OF VENICE
    0 85670 853 4   £8.95

... 60 LE CORBUSIER ARCHIVE
    0 85670 696 5   £8.95

... 61 DESIGNING A HOUSE
    0 85670 888 7   £8.95

... 62 VIENNA DREAM AND REALITY
    0 85670 886 0   £8.95

... 63 NATIONAL GALLERY
    0 85670 884 4   £8.95

... 4/86 MINARDI, ABK, SPEER
    0 85670 894 1   £3.95

... 6/86 KLOTZ, ROB KRIER, STIRLING,
    0 85670 902 6   £3.95

... 7/86 TRADITION, INVENTION, CONVENTION
    0 85670 903 4   £3.95

... 9/86 AMERICAN URBANISM 1
    0 85670 905 0   £3.95

... 64 A HOUSE FOR TODAY
    0 85670 911 5   £8.95

... 66 NEOCLASSICAL ARCHITECTURE
    0 85670 887 9   £8.95

... 67 TRADITION & ARCHITECTURE
    0 85670 890 9   £8.95

... 68 SOVIET ARCHITECTURE
    0 85670 920 4   £8.95

... 69 ARCHITECTURE OF DEMOCRACY
    0 85670 923 9   £8.95

... 70 ENGINEERING & ARCHITECTURE
    0 85670 932 8   £8.95

... 71 THE NEW CLASSICISM
    0 85670 938 7   £8.95

... 72 DECONSTRUCTION IN ARCH
    RP/Sep   0 85670 941 7   £8.95

... 73 JAPANESE ARCHITECTURE
    0 85670 950 6   £8.95

... 74 CONTEMPORARY ARCH
    0 85670 953 0   £8.95

... 75 IMITATION & INNOVATION
    0 85670 954 9   £8.95

... 76 NEW DIRECTIONS IN ARCHITECTURE
    0 85670 992 1   £8.95

... 77 DECONSTRUCTION II
    RP/Sep   0 85670 994 8   £8.95

... 78 DRAWING INTO ARCHITECTURE
    0 85670 997 2   £8.95

... 79 PRINCE CHARLES & ARCH. DEBATE
    1 85490 021 8   £8.95

... 80 CONSTRUCTIVISM & CHERNIKHOV
    1 85490 019 6   £8.95

... 81 RECONSTRUCTION/DECONSTRUCTION
    1 85490 000 5   £8.95

... 82 WEXNER CENTER: EISENMAN
    1 85490 027 7   £8.95

... 83 URBAN CONCEPTS
    0 85670 955 7   £8.95

... 84 NEW ARCHITECTURE
    1 85490 029 3   £8.95

... 85 JAMES STIRLING MICHAEL WILFORD
    1 85490 042 0   £8.95

... 86 THE NEW MODERN AESTHETIC
    1 85490 043 9   £8.95

AD SPECIAL PROFILES

... BRITISH ARCH 82
    0 85670 814 3   £17.50

... LOS ANGELES
    0 85670 785 6   £12.50

... QUINLAN TERRY   0 85670 751 1   £5.95

ART & DESIGN

1990 ANNUAL SUBSCRIPTION RATE (for six double issues inc p&p) *Art & Design*, UK only £39.50. Europe £45. Overseas US$75. Reduced Student Rate: UK £35. Europe £39.50. Overseas US$65. Subscriptions may be backdated to any issue.

... 1 BRITISH ART 20th CENTURY
    0 85670 912 3   £7.95

... 2 POST-MODERN OBJECT
    0 85670 914 X   £7.95

... 3 ABSTRACT ART
    0 85670 919 0   £7.95

... 4 THE POST-AVANT-GARDE
    0 85670 922 0   £7.95

... 5 BRITISH AND AMERICAN ART
    0 85670 930 1   £7.95

... 6 SCULPTURE TODAY
    0 85670 931 X   £7.95

... 7 DAVID HOCKNEY
    0 85670 935 2   £7.95

... 8 THE NEW MODERNISM
    0 85670 940 9   £7.95

... 9 THE CLASSICAL SENSIBILITY
    0 85670 948 4   £7.95

... 10 ART IN THE AGE OF PLURALISM
    0 85670 957 3   £7.95

... 11 BRITISH ART NOW
    0 85670 958 1   £7.95

... 12 THE NEW ROMANTICS
    0 85670 956 5   £7.95

... 13 ITALIAN ART NOW
    0 85670 993 X   £7.95

... 14 40 UNDER 40
    0 85670 995 6   £7.95

... 15 MALEVICH
    0 85670 998 0   £7.95

... 16 NEW YORK NEW ART
    1 85490 004 8   £7.95

... 17 GERMAN ART NOW
    1 85490 023 4   £7.95

... 18 ASPECTS OF MODERN ART
    1 85490 020 X   £7.95

... 19 NEW ART INTERNATIONAL
    1 85490 018 8   £7.95

... 20 ART & THE TECTONIC
    1 85490 037 4   £7.95

... 21 SPIRITUALITY, ART & SCIENCE
    1 85490 038 2   £7.95

ARCHITECTURAL MONOGRAPHS

SUBSCRIPTION RATES (for four issues inc p&p, publication irregular) *Architectural Monographs*, UK only £49.50. Europe £59.50. Overseas US$99.50. Reduced Student Rate: UK £45. Europe £55. Overseas US$89.50. Subscriptions may be backdated to any issue.

... 4 ALVAR AALTO
    0 85670 421 0   £12.95

... 6 EDWIN LUTYENS Rev. Edn
    0 85670 422 9   £12.95

... 6a ROBERT STERN
    NYP/90   1 85490 008 0 PB£14.95

... 8 JOHN SOANE
    0 85670 805 4 PB £12.95

... 9 TERRY FARRELL
    0 85670 842 9 PB£12.95

... 10 RICHARD ROGERS
    0 85670 786 4 PB£12.95

... 11 MIES VAN DER ROHE
    0 85670 685 X PB£12.95

... 12 LE CORBUSIER: Early Work
    0 85670 804 6 PB£12.95

... 13 HASSAN FATHY
    0 85670 918 2 PB£12.95

... 14 TADAO ANDO
    1 85490 007 2 PB£12.95

... C.F.A. VOYSEY
    NYP/90   1 85490 032 3 PB£12.95

UIA JOURNAL

Published in cooperation with the International Union of Architects. SUBSCRIPTION RATES (for four issues inc p&p, publication irregular) *UIA Journal*, UK and Europe £49.50. Overseas US$89.50. Reduced Student Rate: UK and Europe £45. Overseas US$79.50.

... 1 VISION OF THE MODERN
    0 85670 915 8   £12.95

... 2 DECONSTRUCTION – A STUDENT GUIDE
    NYP/Sept   1 85490 034 X   £12.95

JOURNAL OF PHILOSOPHY AND THE VISUAL ARTS

SUBSCRIPTION RATES (for four issues inc p&p, publication irregular) *Journal of Philosophy and the Visual Arts*, UK only £45. Europe £55. Overseas US$89.50. Reduced Student Rate: UK £39.50. Europe £49.50. Overseas US$89.50.

... PHILOSOPHY & THE VISUAL ARTS
    0 85670 966 2   £12.50

... PHILOSOPHY & ARCHITECTURE
    NYP/90   1 85490 016 1   £12.50

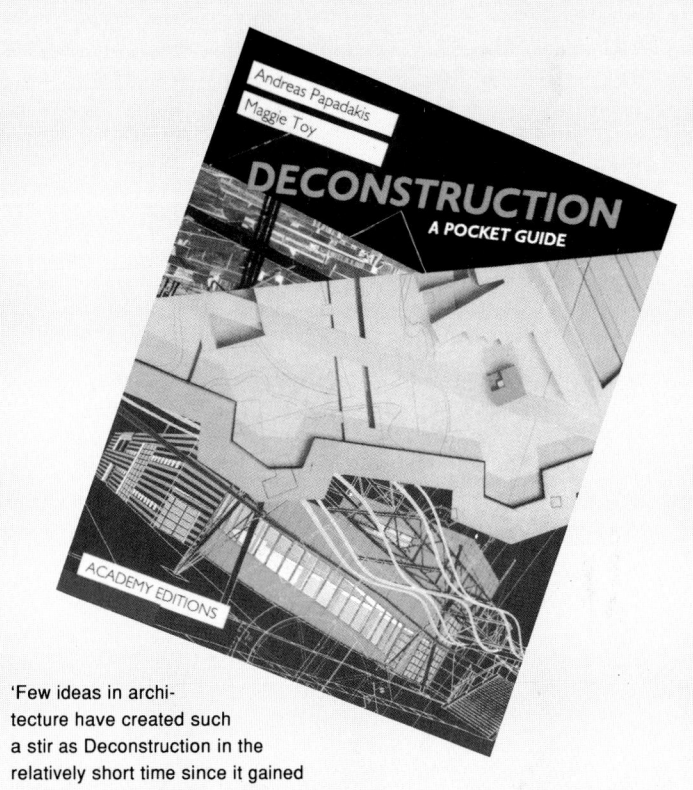

FREDERICK LAW OLMSTEAD: THE PASSIONS OF A PUBLIC ARTIST
by Melvin Kalfus
New York University Press
320 pp B&W illustrations
Cloth $49.50
ISBN 0-8147-4606-3

MOVEMENTS OF MODERNITY: THE CASE OF GLASGOW & ART NOUVEAU
by William Eadie
Routledge
292 pp Cloth £40.00
ISBN 0415 032431

THE ROLE OF TIME FUNCTION IN CITY: SPATIAL STRUCTURES PAST AND PRESENT
by Milos Bobic
Avebury Gower Publishing Company
278 pp B&W illustrations
Cloth £35.00
ISBN 1-85628-005-5

KEYS TO DRAWING
by Bert Dodson
A&C Black
224 pp B&W illustrations
Paperback £12.95
ISBN 0-7136-3252-6

STRUCTURAL DESIGN FOR ARCHITECTS
by Alec Nash
Gower Publishing Company
244 pp B&W ilustrations
Cloth £35.00
ISBN 0-566-02796-8

LIGHT, WIND AND STRUCTURE: THE MYSTERY OF THE MASTER BUILDERS
by Robert Mark
MIT Press
210 pp B&W illustrations
Cloth £17.95
ISBN 0-262-13246-X

DESIGNERS GUIDE TO COLOUR
by Ikuyoshi Shibukawa & Yumi Takahashi
Angus & Robertson
140 pp Paperback £10.95

GLASS ENGRAVING – DRILL TECHNIQUES
by Stuart & Shirley Palmer
Batsford
192 pp B&W illustrations
Cloth £25.00

BUGS BUNNY – FIFTY YEARS ON & ONLY ONE GREY HARE
by Joe Adamson
Pyramid
192 pp Over 400 Col and B&W ills
Cloth £14.95

CHARLES RENNIE MACKINTOSH AND THE MODERN MOVEMENT
by Thomas Howarth
Routledge

336 pp 96 B&W illustrations
Paperback £17.99

A HISTORY OF HOUSING IN NEW YORK CITY
by Richard Plunz
Columbia University Press
442 pp B&W illustrations
$52.00

TOP OF THE CITY – NEW YORK'S HIDDEN ROOFTOP WORLD
by Laura Rosen
Thames & Hudson
168 pp Paperback £14.95

THE CHALLENGE OF LANDSCAPE PAINTING
by Ian Simpson
Collins
160 pp Cloth £16.95

GIO PONTI – THE COMPLETE WORK 1923-1978
by Lisa Licitra Ponti
Thames & Hudson
288 pp Cloth £45.00

SIMPLIFIED DESIGN OF STEEL STRUCTURES
by Harry Parker – James Ambrose
Wiley Interscience
438 pp Cloth £32.15

MODELLING OBJECTS AND ENVIRONMENTS
by Yehuda E Kalay
Wiley Interscience
402 pp Cloth £62.15

FINNISH WOODEN CHURCH
by Lars Petterson
Museum of Finnish Architecture
160 pp Paperback

RENAISSANCE AND BAROQUE
by E James Mundy
Cambridge University Press
316 pp Cloth £45.00

SV DICTIONARY No B 3 4: CIVIL ENGINEERING & BUILDING CONSTRUCTION
English – Spanish
Schnellmann Verlag Widnau/ Switzerland
120 pp Paperback

PRAHA 19. A20 STOLETI
by Jiri Kohout – Jiri Vancura
SNTL
290 pp Cloth

SLIPS AND SLIPWARE – THE COMPLETE POTTER
by Anthony Phillips
Batsford
96 pp Col and B&W illustrations
Cloth £12.95

ANIMAL FORMS AND FIGURES – THE COMPLETE POTTER
by Rosemary Wren

Batsford
96 pp Col and B&W illustrations
Cloth £ 12.95

THE ENCYCLOPEDIA OF POTTERY TECHNIQUES
by Peter Cosentino
Headline
192 pp col illustrations
Cloth £14.95

POST ISLAMIC CLASSICISM
by Kanan Makiya
Saqi Books
160 pp col and B&W illustrations
Cloth £35.00

DOMESTIC ARCHITECTURE AND USE OF SPACE
by Susan Kent
Cambrdige
192 pp Cloth £30.00

FRANK GEHRY – VITRA DESIGN MUSEUM
Boissiere – Filler
Thames & Hudson
102 pp Paperback £15.00

THE WATTS TOWERS OF LOS ANGELES
by Leon Whiteson
Mosaic Press
96 pp
Paperback $17.95 Cloth $24.95

CARLO SCARPA & CASTELVECCHIO
by Richard Murphy
Butterworth Architecture
198 pp Cloth

AWARD FOR EUROPEAN ARCHITECTURE: MIES VAN DER ROHE
Butterworth Architecture
128 pp Paperback £19.95

NEW YORK ARCHITECTURE
by Heinrich Klotz
Rizzoli
336 pp Cloth

THE PENCIL: A HISTORY
by Henry Petroski
Faber & Faber
434 pp Cloth £14.99

CAST IRON (SHIRE ALBUM 250)
by Jacqueline Fearn
Shire Publications
Paperback £1.95

MODERNISM IN DESIGN
by Paul Greenhalgh
Reakton Books
256 pp 60 illustrations
Paperback £9.95 Cloth £23.00

VISUAL ILLUSIONS – PICTURES OF PERCEPTION
by Nicholas Wade
Lawrence Erlbaum Assoc. Ltd
288pp Cloth £24.95

THE ECONOMICS OF BUILDING
by Robert E Johnson
Wiley Interscience
248 pp Paperback & Cloth

THE ROMANTIC ENGLISH GARDEN
by Jane Taylor
Weidenfeld & Nicolson
118 pp Cloth £12.95

ICONS
by T Talbot Rice
Studio Editions
144 pp Cloth £9.95

ITALIAN LIVING DESIGN
by Guiseppe Raimondi
Taurus Parke Books
288 pp Cloth £24.95

THE GHETTO OF VENICE
by Roberto Curiel – Bernard Dov Cooperman
Taurus Parke Books
176 pp Cloth

VAN GOGH – THE MASTERWORKS
William Feaver
Studio Editions
144 pp Cloth

TURNER
by Eric Shanes
Studio Editions
144 pp Cloth

THE DESIGN DIMENSION
by Christopher Lorenz
Blackwell
172 Pages Paperback £12.95

LANDSCAPE DESIGN GUIDE VOL1 & 2: SOFT LANDSCAPE & HARD LANDSCAPE
by Adrian Lisney & Ken Fieldhouse
Gower
168 & 192pp Cloth £35.00 each

WOMEN ENGRAVERS
by Patricia Jaffe
Virago Press
128 pp Paperback £9.99

THE BACH FLOWER REMEDIES STEP BY STEP
by Judy Howard
C W Daniel
68 pp Paperback £2.95

FASTING THE BUCHINGER METHOD
by C W Daniel
80 pp Paperback

BALKAN HOURS
by Richard Bassett
John Murray
148 pp Cloth £14.95

LOTUS INTERNATIONAL No 65
Electa
144pp Paperback